HOW TO GET WHAT YOU WANT FROM GOD

HOW TO GET WHAT YOU WANT FROM GOD

Herbert F. Smith, S.J.

Our Sunday Visitor, Inc.
Huntington, Indiana 46750

Imprimi Potest:
Very Rev. Joseph A. Panuska, S.J., Maryland Prov. Soc. Jesu
Baltimore, Md., August 4, 1978

Nihil Obstat:
Msgr. James McGrath
Censor Librorum

Imprimatur:
✠John Cardinal Krol
Archbishop of Philadelphia
April 20, 1979

Scripture quotes (except when identified by NAT or J) are from the *Revised Standard Version of the Bible*, copyright 1946, 1952, ©1971, 1973 by the National Council of Churches of Christ, New York, N.Y. NAT signifies the New American Translation (*The New American Bible*, copyright ©1970 by the Confraternity of Christian Doctrine, Washington, D.C.); J signifies *The Jerusalem Bible*, copyright ©1966 by Darton, Longman and Todd, Ltd., London, and Doubleday and Co., Inc., New York. Photos are by the author, except for the photo on page 38 by John A. Zierten. If we have unwittingly infringed copyright with any other material in this book, we sincerely apologize and request notification by the copyright owner.

Copyright ©1979 by Our Sunday Visitor, Inc.

All rights reserved. No part of this book may be reproduced or copied in any form or by any means — graphic, electronic, or mechanical, including photocopying, recording, taping, or information storage and retrieval systems — without written permission of the publisher.

ISBN: 0-87973-632-1
Library of Congress Catalog Card Number: 79-87927

Design by James E. McIlrath

Published, printed, and bound in the United States of America

*For my Mothers,
Mary and Clara*

Contents

Foreword	9
PART ONE	11
1. Jesus Prayer for the Well and the Sick	13
2. New Life for the Our Father	15
3. How to Destroy Your Enemies	16
4. A Pattern for Personhood	19
5. Why Is God So Hidden	20
6. Right Attitude Toward a Pregnant Single Girl	23
7. How to Pray Like Mary	25
8. Set Sail for a More Satisfying Life Today	27
9. The Body Language of Religion	29
PART TWO	33
10. The Parable of the Key	35
11. Light Up Your Faith	37
12. Sight Without Eyes	39
13. The Pattern of Our Love	41
14. No Devotion for Losers	44
15. The Easter Christ in Our Lives	45
16. This Is to Know Jesus	47
17. The Fourth of July and the Mass	50
18. The Catholic and the Common Good	53
19. Friends of the Wedding	55

PART THREE	57
20. The Enigma of God	59
21. Trailblazer of the Sacred Heart Devotion	62
22. The Love You Save May Be Your Own	64
23. Sweet Mystery of Life	66
24. Confession Is Too Easy	68
25. The Wonder of Christmas	70
26. I Am a Sinner	72
27. How to Get What You Want from God	76
PART FOUR	79
28. Marriage Without Divorce	81
29. Is Patriotism a Museum Piece?	85
30. Thank God for the Pope!	89
31. Questions Men Ask God	92
32. How Can I Stop Being Angry?	96
33. Don't Waste Your Sufferings!	100
34. Why Do I Need the Church?	102
35. Frequent Confession Yesterday, Today, and Tomorrow	104
PART FIVE	109
36. Instant Independence	111
37. Prayer Is Not for Simpletons	113
38. The Mystery of Mysteries	116
39. Love Yourself as Your Neighbor	118
40. Spiritual Monkey Children	121
41. Little Helps to Love	123
42. Improving Our Prayer of Petition	126
43. The Lamb Who Is Shepherd	128
44. Woman of Women	130
45. The Mystery of Happiness	132
46. What's It All About, Lord?	134
47. Making Decisions in the Lord	136

PART SIX	139
48. The Ever-Human Jesus	141
49. Dereliction	143
50. Saint Joseph and Fatherhood	147
51. Mercy We Can Count On	150
52. Death of a Christian	153
53. A Secret of Patience	156
54. Death and Resurrection	158
55. Who's Afraid of the Golden Rule?	161
56. Big Little Things	165
57. A Saint in the Making	168

Foreword

How-to-do-it books are always popular because always needed. This is a how-to-do-it book: how to pray, how to ask favors of God, how to grow in patience, in kindness, in knowledge of God. It is a book of little helps: little helps to love, to growth, to peace, to happiness.

How-to-do-it books should get at the gist of things simply and in the vernacular of the day. In this book I try to speak with that simplicity. I try to do it in terms of our current idioms and interests and with the help of pictures that save a thousand words. The pictures helped to keep the book little, and for that we should all be grateful.

Herbert Francis Smith, S.J.

PART 1

1. The Jesus Prayer for the Well and the Sick

Have you ever felt a longing to pray better and more frequently? Have you ever felt the need for a form of prayer that can really help you when you are sick or in pain?

Jesus says to us: 'Watch at all times, praying that you may have strength. . . .'" Many Christians through the ages have tried to obey these words, and they have devised some ingenious methods to help us pray. One of the simplest and most effective of these methods is called THE JESUS PRAYER.

The account of THE JESUS PRAYER begins with the story of a pilgrim wandering through Russia many years ago, searching for a wise guide who could teach him how to pray constantly. He soon met a priest who told him about THE JESUS PRAYER.

The priest said: "The continuous interior prayer of Jesus is a constant, uninterrupted calling upon the divine Name of Jesus with lips in spirit, and in heart. The words you say are: LORD JESUS CHRIST, HAVE MERCY ON ME."

The pilgrim began repeating this prayer hundreds of times a day. He soon felt the love of Jesus burning in his heart.

The pilgrim's experience is inspiring, but he soon had the problem of distraction. How could he keep his mind on THE JESUS PRAYER? He went back to his teacher, who answered by taking up a book called the *Philokalia*, and reading the following passage: "The power of pronouncing words is in the throat. Reject all other thoughts, and allow the throat to repeat only: LORD JESUS CHRIST, HAVE MERCY ON ME."

Remarkably enough, this advice from the *Philokalia* is confirmed by a modern psychologist, who wrote that man cannot think without forming words in his throat. By controlling the words his throat forms, man controls his thoughts.

To apply this knowledge to THE JESUS PRAYER, a Christian focuses his attention on his throat, and allows it to form only the words, LORD JESUS CHRIST, HAVE MERCY ON ME. He does this repeatedly. While doing it, he thinks of Jesus entering his throat. When he has practiced this for days or weeks, and mastered it, he goes on to the second step. He focuses attention on his mind, and brings Jesus there by repeating THE JESUS PRAYER. Third, he focuses on his heart, and repeats, inviting Jesus into his heart. Fourth, he focuses on his spirit, and repeats, inviting Jesus to enter. Then, as often as he wants, he repeats the whole, focusing in turn on throat, mind, heart, and spirit, saying THE JESUS PRAYER each time.

One can make special application of THE JESUS PRAYER for the sick. If one has a headache, for instance, he focuses on that and repeats THE JESUS PRAYER, so the Divine Physician can enter and heal. He can do the same for pain or sickness in any part of the body. The Russian pilgrim reports on an alcoholic who conquered his alcoholism by the use of THE JESUS PRAYER.

Variations of THE JESUS PRAYER can be created. The following is one example: Each time he breathes in, the Christian says the Name JESUS, breathing His Divine love into himself. Each time he breathes out, he says MARY, giving to her and to all creatures his love, which God is giving him.

2. New Life for the Our Father

Is there any way to revitalize familiar prayers we repeatedly say, prayers like the OUR FATHER *and the* HAIL MARY? *How can a person get out of the habit of rattling off these prayers without attention or devotion?*

Everything needs care. Plants need watering, cars need servicing, people need love. But does it ever occur to us that even the OUR FATHER needs care and maintenance? If we just rattle off the OUR FATHER each time we use it, it seems to dry up, and give us no nourishment after a while. That is because the OUR FATHER needs care itself, just as a plant needs rain. We give that care to the OUR FATHER by giving it the dew and the rain of meditation, by meditating on each word and phrase.

To learn how to give new life to the OUR FATHER, and to all vocal prayers, we make a meditation on the OUR FATHER: "Our Father," we begin, and we think about those two words. Father. We know our father as the head of our family, the one who, with our mother, has given us life. We know God because we are made in His image and likeness. And He has given us a human father, who is made like to Him. And our fathers, particularly, can know God by knowing what they are, what they have done; by meditating on how they have brought a family into being, just as God the Father has brought the whole human family and the whole universe into being. And mothers, too, can meditate on God by thinking on their own experience of motherhood, for God is both Father and Mother of all creation, and the motherly experience of giving and nourishing life tells them much about the nature of God our Creator.

We don't just say "Father," for Jesus has taught us to say "Our Father." And so we reflect on how God, who has given us being, has also given us Himself to be ours, as we are His. And so we bless Him and say, "Hallowed be thy name." We say "Thy kingdom come," for we yearn for His fatherly care to be felt by us to the full. And so as Jesus taught us, we go on praying and meditating on this prayer.

There is an especially easy way to do this kind of meditation, a way which makes use of the rhythm of one's own body. One of the basic rhythms in the universe is breathing, and one of the most personal rhythms in the universe is one's own breathing. So each time he breathes in, the meditator says one phrase of the OUR FATHER, and he thinks of the meaning of that phrase, for one whole breath; and on his next breath, he goes on to the next phrase of the OUR FATHER, and thus he continues through the whole of the prayer. The one who tries this will discover that, as his breathing gives him life, this way of praying will breathe new life into the OUR FATHER.

3. How to Destroy Your Enemies

Is there enmity or hostility in your life? Are there some clear and simple ways of thinking and acting that can help us live in peace?

All of us have trouble getting along with others at times. Not uncommonly, people don't get along well even with their best friends. Marriages shatter, and good friends turn into bitter enemies. These terrible breakups are the evil fruit of bad attitudes that we ought to look at and change before it is too late.

Some parents get hostile toward a slow or disobedient child. The word *hostile* comes from the Latin word *hostis*, which means *the enemy*! Husbands and wives frequently show hostility toward one another for petty reasons.

How can we root this hostility out of our lives? What breeds hostility? The answer is, *anger*. Anger leads us to be destructive, to be the enemy of the one who causes it. Anger is an attack upon the faults and failings of another. We even get

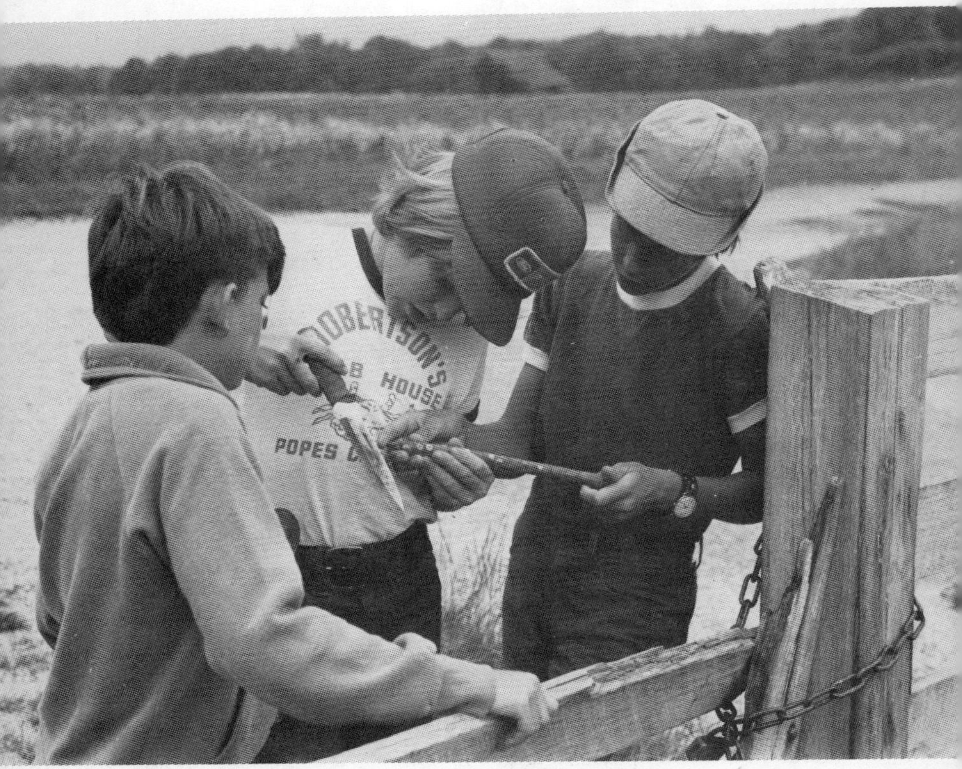
HOUSE
POPES

angry with God, who has no faults and failings, but who sometimes displeases us.

This gives us a hint of the real root of anger and hostility. The root is our *impatience* — that is, our *unwillingness to suffer*. The moment someone we love causes us discomfort, we let our selfishness overcome our love. We lash out to stop the hurt, in turn hurting the one we love. For a moment, we stop loving. Yet Jesus said: "Love your enemies." *Even* your enemies. And Shakespeare wrote: "Love is not love/which alters when it alteration finds. . . ."

Jesus not only told us what to do to overcome anger and hostility. He did it Himself first. Even while Judas was in the act of betrayal, Jesus still addressed him as a friend and said: "Friend, why are you here?" Jesus was willing to suffer rather than stop loving. He was willing to endure those who acted as His enemies rather than destroy them. There was only one thing Jesus was willing to destroy in His enemies, and that was their *enmity*. And He did that not by violence, but by love. Even as Jesus was being nailed to the cross by us rebellious and hostile sinners He kept saying, "Father, forgive them. . . ."

During the Civil War, a Southern woman begged President Lincoln to free her captured son. She had no support and needed him to work the plantation. Lincoln freed him. A northern woman who heard of it stormed up to the President with the words: "Mr. President! You don't free your enemy, you destroy him!" Lincoln replied: "Madam, if I make my enemy my friend, don't I destroy my *enemy*?"

If we have even one enemy, it is one too many to hold in a heart like Christ's. Some may call us their enemy, but we should not call them ours.

To avoid making enemies, we should cultivate the following helps to friendliness. First, adopt the heart of Jesus, which simply refuses to have enemies. Second, be ready to suffer to make love grow. Third, don't get sullen and depressed when offended. Fourth, be patient with the self when anger comes, as it will at times. Fifth, pray for those who are unkind or unjust. God's grace works wonders.

If we do these things we will destroy our enemies by making them our friends.

4. A Pattern for Personhood

Are the Ten Commandments enough to guide our lives? Is something better needed?

Life is like a TV set. The outside looks neat, but the inside is a jungle of wires! How can anyone make anything of it? The answer is that, in fact, even a TV service engineer needs a wiring diagram, or schematic, to work on that jungle efficiently. We need a pattern for everything we want to understand or make. We need blueprints, mock-ups, architectural drawings. One of my earliest memories is that of my mother, kneeling on the floor, cutting cloth to a full-sized pattern.

For life, too, we need patterns to guide us. The poet Wordsworth has said: "The Child is father of the Man. . . ." That is, each of us has to fashion our adulthood from our childhood, and our future from our present. To a great extent, each of us is the product of our own past actions. We are each engaged in self-making activity. If that is true, we must have a pattern for what we want to become. If we don't have one, we will almost certainly turn out to be *a mess*.

There is a history to the human pattern. Adam and Eve had themselves for a pattern, for God gave them unsullied innocence, a perfect intellect, and a free will. But they ruined all that, and darkness fell over the earth. There was no longer any clear pattern for personhood.

God gave the Jews the Ten Commandments for a pattern. They were proud of it, but they didn't keep the Commandments. The Commandments lightened the eyes, but didn't warm the heart. It is hard to march through life in the wake of two cold stone tablets!

Those Ten Commandments were only an interim pattern. God has now given us the definitive one. He has sent us His Son, who became flesh, a human being, one of us. Now at last we have the perfect pattern for personhood — not cold stone, but warm human nature like ours, only without sin, without disobedience. Jesus is our pattern, our blueprint, our schematic. To Philip, His Apostle, He said: "I *am* the Way." Jesus is the godlike man, because Jesus *is* God-become-also-Man. Jesus said to Philip: "He who sees me sees the Father." The humanity of Jesus is the finite version of God.

What a treasure we have in Jesus Christ! We no longer walk in darkness. We can read the Gospels, meditate on the life of Jesus, talk to Jesus in prayer, receive Him in Holy Communion. We can develop devotion to His Sacred Heart — the pattern for ours. When we take Jesus for our pattern, we are saved not only from darkness but from eternal death, for Jesus is not only light but life.

5. Why Is God So Hidden?

Why is it that unbelievers who lived in the age when the psalmist wrote could say sarcastically, "Where is his God?"? Why is it that unbelievers of our own day can say cynically, "God is dead"?

Recently I saw a frothy song-and-dance movie called "The Young Girls of Rochefort." I found it had a simple message we of this hurried, harassed, and mechanized age badly need. The movie reminded me that love is a poem. Love is a pageant. Love is a ritual. Take away singing and dancing, take away pageantry and ritual, and you mutilate love.

Even the animals tell us it is so. The fish, the mammals,

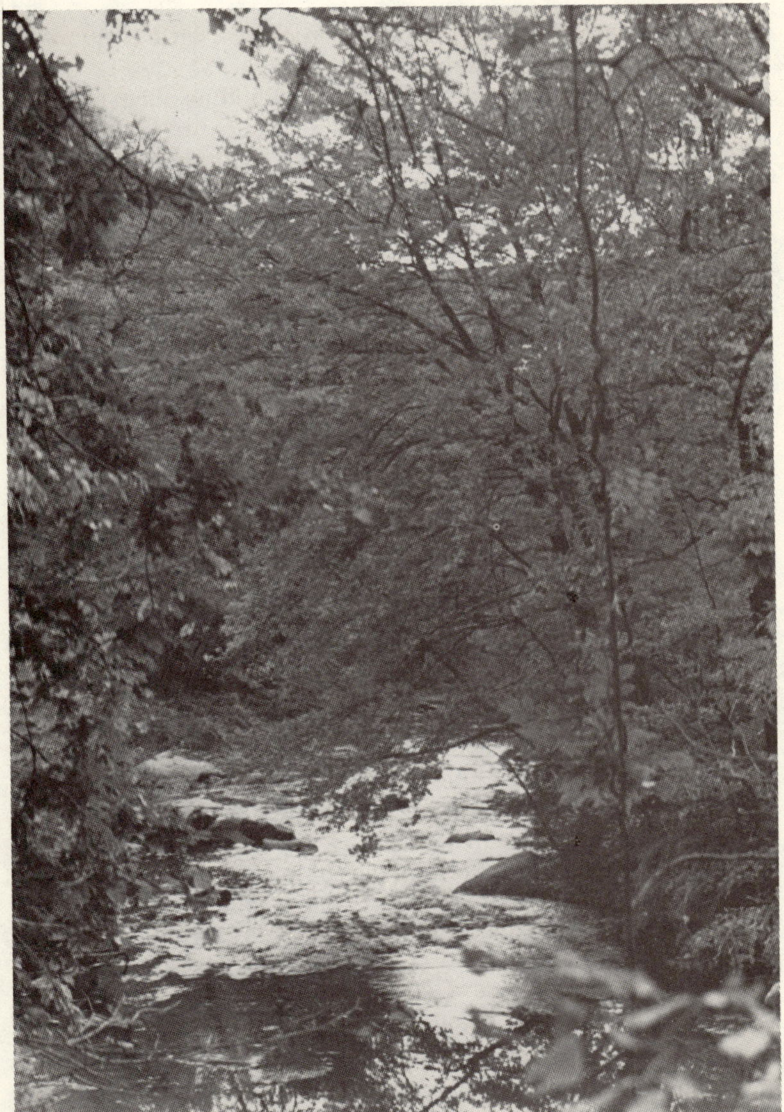

and the singing birds approach one another in patient rituals of courtship. Love is not violent.

What does this poetic nature of love tell us about the God who created both us and the animals? It ought to tell us something, for the Bible itself tells us that God reveals Himself through His works.

I think this mystery of love helps us to solve a riddle about which we have all wondered. It tells us why God is so hidden. It is because He too needs to reveal Himself patiently through the ritual of love.

What would happen, for instance, if God should suddenly burst upon us in all His grandeur and power? He might terrify us the way the Israelites were terrified by the thunder and lightning over Mount Sinai, so that they did not want to go near God.

I think God hides Himself from us because if He should suddenly approach us openly in all His innocence and unconditional love, it would destroy us. What I mean is very hard to explain. Nothing makes us feel so unworthy, so "wiped out," as being offered love and friendship by one whose shoes we are not worthy to take off, as John the Baptist put it.

There is nothing so demanding of us as one who loves us and demands nothing. There is no one who can make our own nothingness crush us so completely as one who tenderly forgives us times without number and asks nothing in return. One who gives so completely is more demanding than any moral code, because by demanding nothing he awakens us to making demands on ourselves, the demands of love.

Without even wanting to do so, one who loves us in perfect innocence exposes our self-centeredness. The radiance of his unconditional love shames the shoddy calculations we called love.

The mystics, who are so sensitive to God's love and God's presence, show us how burdensome it can be if God does not approach us slowly, gently, veiled in the mystery of faith, giving us time to get used to our poverty and His holiness. Even the psalmist once got so burdened by his feeling of worthlessness in the presence of God's holiness that he said to God: "Look away from me, that I may know gladness, before I depart and be no more!" A modern man might say: "Look away, God, so that I can exaggerate and lie and cheat a little, and drink heavy and spit tobacco juice like my friends!"

O God, You are a hidden God because You are such a gentle God. We thank You for being a hidden God. We ask You to approach us slowly, gently, with patient understanding, until we can live comfortably with You, and can no longer live without You. Then at last You can show us Your glory.

6. Right Attitude Toward a Pregnant Single Girl

What attitude do you have toward a girl who conceives a child out of wedlock? Is it a Christian attitude?

In a recent twenty-five year period, births out of wedlock nearly tripled. By 1964, almost three hundred thousand girls were bearing children out of wedlock each year. That means that most of us sooner or later have manifested to such a girl our reaction to her dilemma.

How should we treat her? How can we deal with her according to the Heart of Christ? In answer, I would like to make three statements which I think ought to guide our conduct. First I will make the statements, then I will consider each one.

Here are the three statements: Rejection is not Christian. Acceptance is not approval. Marriage is not always a solution. Now let us consider each one.

First: Rejection is not Christian. Whatever the girl did wrong, she is doing nothing wrong now. Now she needs our love and mercy, not our condemnation. If we are not kind and understanding, we may be guilty of driving her to worse sin, even to abortion. Is it right to drive a human being to correct an act of passion by committing an act of murder? The only right way is to accept her with understanding.

Second: Acceptance is not approval. When God accepts us after we have sinned, we do not take it as approval of the sin. Acceptance is forgiveness, not approval. We ought to remember how kind Jesus was to the adulterous woman who was brought to Him. On that occasion, Jesus posed a dilemma for us. Either we ourselves are sinners, and have no right to self-righteously condemn another whose sin happens not to be hidden; or, like Jesus, we are sinless, and have no desire to condemn but only to help.

A girl who was single and pregnant came to me for guidance. I told her that by her brave acceptance of the situation she was pleasing God very much, and was more than atoning for her weakness.

Third: Marriage is not always a solution. Marriage is a sacred and perpetual commitment, not a Band-Aid to hide a morally wrong act, and not a device to give a legal name. For the Christian who accepts the word of Christ and His Church, marriage is for life. Unless the couple want to marry, marriage will be no solution, as marriage counselors know from experience. Shotgun weddings add more evils than they take away. If the couple want to marry, surely it would be terribly wrong for anyone to prevent them, unless they are marrying for the wrong motive. If they do not want to marry, it would be equally wrong to force them. Both the boy and the girl should be called on to take their share of responsibility toward the child conceived, but they should not be asked to enter a marriage which one or the other may resent for a lifetime.

All sin and loss of self-control brings sorrow and burdens. When that sorrow takes the form of a girl who has to bear her child without the comfort of a loving husband, the Heart of Christ calls us to an understanding acceptance of her, and a readiness to help her find the most human and Christian way of caring for her child.

7. How to Pray Like Mary

We Catholics often ask Mary, the Mother of Jesus, to pray for us, but would it not be better if we asked her to teach us to pray? Will she not gladly help us to fulfill her Son's instruction to pray always?

We often think of prayer as asking things of God, or thinking things about God, or saying things to God, but Mary's prayer shows us prayer is much more.

The first time the girl Mary surfaces in history is at the Annunciation, and already then she shows the first-fruits of prayer, humility and obedience. She calls herself the slave, the handmaid, of God, and that is what she was. That is what every one of us who wishes to pray must be. We must acknowledge our relationship of creaturehood to the great Lord and Master of Creation. Mary teaches us to imitate her own humble obedience by her words at Cana in Galilee! "Do whatever He tells you."

In our prayer, we ought to examine whether we are really in fact God's obedient servants. We ought to do that every day. I feel certain Mary did.

After the birth of Jesus, Mary lived with Him, wondered at the things that happened to Him, and kept her mind and heart occupied trying to understand Him better. In all of this, Mary teaches us the secret of prayer, which is to keep Jesus daily before the eyes of our soul.

The practice of prayer raised Mary to a high level of consciousness. It enhanced her awareness of God's personal relationship to her, and of His gifts to all men, and of His control over all history. The resulting consolation of feeling herself always in God's hand changed sorrow to joy, and made her burst forth in a song of praise which shows that Mary had not only knowledge of the past and the present, but even the future: "My soul magnifies the Lord, and my spirit rejoices in God my Savior . . . all generations will call me blessed." We

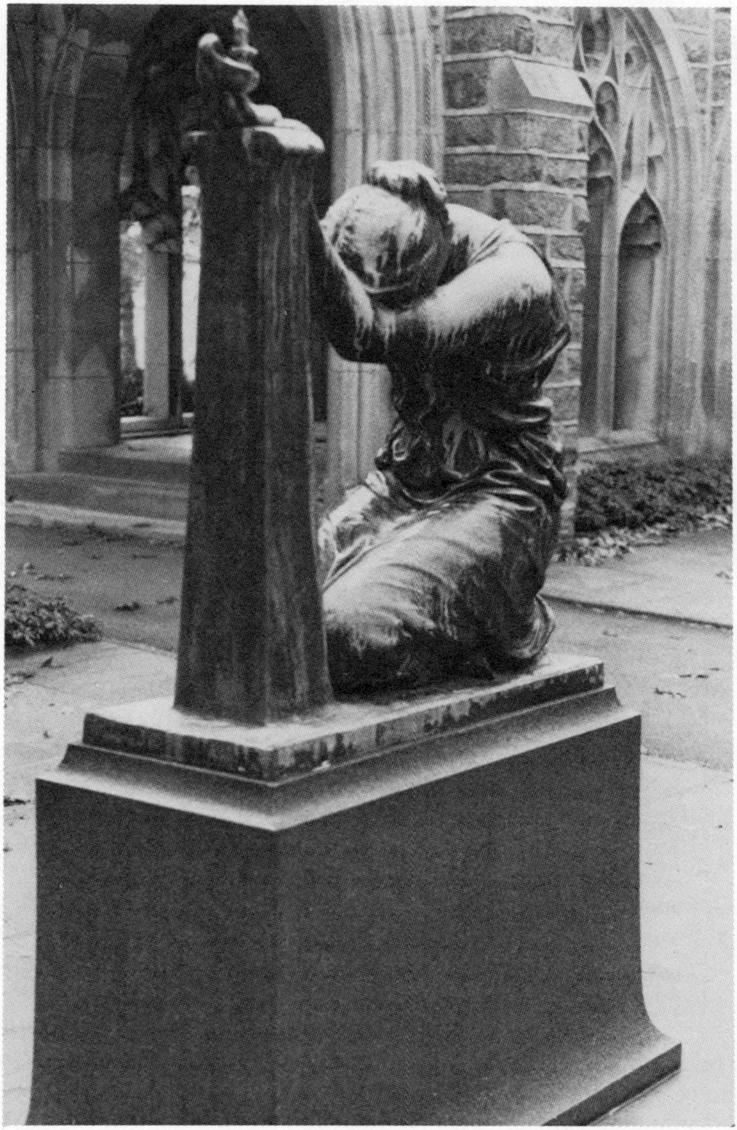

too, if we meditate on the word of God and His promises, will gain understanding of our times, and hope in God's saving work in history.

Even so, Mary was sometimes stunned by the ways of her Divine Son, and of His Father. When after three days she found her boy in the temple, where He had stayed without explanation, we wrung out of her the words: "Son, why have You done this to us?" Mary's life teaches us that even through prayer we should not expect to understand why God permits certain things to happen in our lives. The business of our heavenly Father is sometimes just too great for our grasp.

Perhaps Mary's prayer at the foot of the cross teaches us the most. Her prayer there was silence and presence. Words would have spoiled her communion with her Son in His suffering. Sometimes in our prayer, too, we are called simply to spend time with God, without words. Mary may have seemed to do nothing there, but her silent presence was a total gift of self to Jesus. He accepted her gift, and used it by giving her to John and to all of us: "Behold your Mother." From then on, she took on her shoulders His work. Like Mary, we should find our prayer a time when we make ourselves available to Jesus, so that when we come out of our prayer, we undertake His works and sufferings for the sake of His people and the coming of His kingdom. And for that coming He Himself taught us to pray.

8. Set Sail for a More Satisfying Life Today

Do you sometimes feel your life with mate and children is not enough? Do you feel guilty about these feelings, or do you realize they may be a call to a fuller life?

Millions of people nowadays feel a leaden sense of emptiness and have no idea why. The problem is often not their marriage. In fact they love their mates and children — so much so that these feelings of emptiness make them feel guilty, as if such feelings were a betrayal of their loved ones. Then, too, they may like their work, and they may go to church on Sunday — yet this emptiness persists.

If they are asked whether they pray, they are likely to answer indignantly, "Of course!"

Yet the question needs to be asked, and pursued: Do we pray? Do we know what adult prayer really is? Are we aware our lives can become healthier and happier simply by making a change in the inner spaces of our lives? The sense of not being fulfilled may have nothing to do with the outer affairs of life. It is more likely a spiritual pain signaling spiritual sickness, as bodily pain signals bodily sickness.

Someone might respond: "Well, I do pray. I ask God for things and I say my prayers."

Let us look at that answer: "I ask God for things." That would be prayer of petition. It is good prayer, it is necessary prayer, but it is not enough. What if husbands and wives never spoke to one another except to ask for something? Prayer of petition is only a part of our life of prayer, which is our life with God. Such a poverty-stricken relationship with God will leave us empty, unfulfilled.

Our respondent may add: "But I also told you: I say my prayers. For instance, I say the Our Father every day, and blessings at meals."

To expose the inadequacy of such prayer, let me pose a question: What if a husband spoke to his wife and children only once or twice a day, and did it in the same words every day? Would not the whole situation be inhuman?

Well, what about our relationship with God? Don't we have to keep it as warm and living and human as we can? Living prayer helps us do that. Living prayer is companionship with God. Once we begin enjoying His daily companionship, emptiness is gone, and happiness comes.

Think of Jesus during His time on earth. He would go up on a mountain and spend whole nights in the company of the heavenly Father, by prayer.

How can we get deeper into prayer? One simple way will make a beginning. Take the Gospels, and read just a few words, and then be still, letting God tell you in your heart what He wants these words to mean to you. When a meaning comes to you, tell Him in your own words what that meaning is. Then go on to the next few words.

This practice helps us to learn to listen to God, as well as speak to Him in our own words. It makes prayer a two-way communication. It brings us close to God. And once we find we are getting closer to God, our lives will give us the satisfaction that only God can give.

9. The Body Language of Religion

Are words enough to tell God of our love? Or is there a more eloquent language?

Almost all of us find it easy and pleasant to talk. This gives rise to the idea that communication should be easy. Yet misunderstanding is one of the most widespread of human problems. One reason is that we depend too much on talk — talk is cheap — and too little on our more self-giving forms of communication. A look of sympathy often says more than words ever can. Or sometimes we reach out spontaneously to take the hand of one in trouble, and it does more good than all our words.

These gestures are familiar to all of us, but recently someone has brightly called them "body language" because of their eloquence. This body language has long been used in talking to

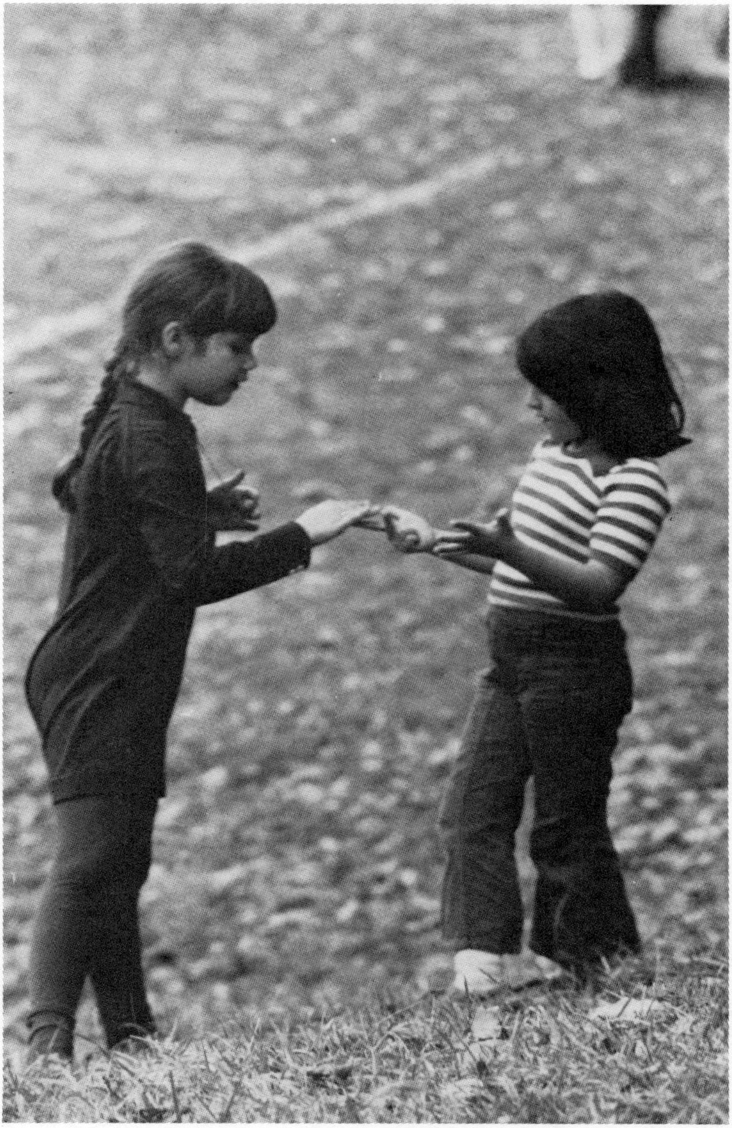

God: at Mass we genuflect and kneel to God; the priest lifts his hands to the Lord in hope and kisses the altar, which symbolizes His presence. And together we strike our breasts in sorrow, as though to drive evil from our hearts and make them more like Christ's.

But what may be religion's most eloquent body language is suffering. Suffering is not good in itself, but it can be put to good use. We can make it speak more eloquently than Shakespeare, and more convincingly than angels. It was an evil thing when men crucified Jesus, but how eloquently His body speaks to us from the cross! It says to me: "I have loved you and delivered myself up for you."

Men often refused to believe in God's love until God became a man and spoke to us of His love through the body language of His suffering. Jesus Himself spoke of a connection between love and the language of bodily suffering when He said: "Greater love than this no man has, that a man lay down his life for his friends"; and the very next day He laid down His life for us.

Think of soldiers in war speaking to their country of their love by their deprivations and wounds and death. Think of fathers speaking of love to their wives and children through bodies grown tired and worn in earning their living. Think of mothers suffering to give birth to their children, and wearing out their bodies in caring for them.

Some of us are not skilled at reading these sacrifices and sufferings as the body language of love. Some of us are not good at expressing our love for God and man through the body language of suffering. When we have to do without, when we are hurt or sick, we need not curse or complain; we can see in these things opportunities to speak of our love. At one time, it is a chance to speak with understanding love for a husband who can't find a job; at another, it is an opportunity to speak with understanding love to God, who is offering the privilege of sharing the redemptive sufferings of Jesus.

We may not understand why God permits so much suffering, but we can understand this much: that when we suffer with loving trust in Him, He will not fail to hear the body language of our love for Him — and how happy He will be that we return the message of love He sends us from the cross!

Christ came to do away with suffering by enduring it Himself, and He came to do away with death by dying and rising from the dead. We become like Christ when we work to remove as much suffering from the lives of others as we can. There is suffering in doing it, but that suffering is the opportunity to speak the body language of love for God and man.

PART 2

10. The Parable of the Key

Can parables still lead us to think thoughts of faith and of life?

A man with shining eyes used to go about the city asking people, "Where are you going?" Some said, "Nowhere," and to them he replied, "But shouldn't you be?" Some said, "I don't know," and to them he said, "I will tell you." To all he gave a very large key, which he explained as follows: "This key will help you to know where you are going, and it will give you entrance when you get there. When you get hungry, you must eat some of the key, no matter what it tastes like. Never, never throw this key away."

Some laughed in his face and threw the key at him. Others carried it away, but it was clumsy, and when they couldn't put it in purse or pocket conveniently and forget it, they threw it in the mud. Some saw that the key was crimson on one side and white on the other, and asked what this meant. He said only that if the crimson or white became discolored, or the equal-sided triangle (which they had not noticed) became marred, the key would no longer work unless it were painstakingly cleaned.

All who received the key went on the journey of life. When they became hungry, those who still had the key would remember the words of the man with the shining eyes and take a bite of the key. To some the key tasted like bread and wine, and it filled them with strength; to others, the key tasted bitter; some of these threw the key away, but some continued to eat it even though it was bitter, for they found it gave them strength for their journey, and helped their eyes to see better where they were going in the gathering darkness; and they discovered that the key began to taste sweet for them too.

Finally all came to the end of their journey and appeared before a golden door that revolved and led to a golden corridor out of which light and laughter floated into the darkness (for it was suddenly growing dark with a strange darkness that looked as though it would never grow light again). Those who had eaten their key on the journey found the revolving door turned easily for them, as though they had become the key. Those who had eaten part of the key found the revolving door turned a little for them, and turned the rest of the way when they inserted the remainder of the key. Those who had refused to eat the key because it was bitter, and those who had allowed their key to lose its crimson and white and its delicate triangle, and those who had thrown away their keys, all found that the revolving door would not budge for them. They could not enter the golden corridor no matter how much they cursed the key and the turnstile, and the man with the shining eyes, and those who had entered so gaily. Suddenly, they all looked up, startled. All whose keys would work had entered, and now beautiful music emanated from the golden corridor — and the light became a hundred times more beautiful than before, and gasps of wonder and cries of joy came from the golden corridor — and then the lovely sounds and the radiant glow began to fade, as though a door were slowly being closed, and all went black outside. And there were those who were inside, and those who were outside. "He who has ears to hear, let him hear!"

11. Light Up Your Faith

Is religious faith really a leap into the dark as some say? Is it a foolish hope, or the wisest and most reasonable hope of all?

If you are reading this, you are not in Russia or China — or at least you are not reading it in a book published in Russia or China. Why? Because no one is permitted publicly to teach his faith in such countries. It is legal to attack religion there, but not to teach religion.

The reason is that these countries condemn religion as a false, even irrational thing. The state considers itself bound to protect its people from such "superstitions." But let me ask a question: Is the state protecting people or is it protecting itself from the people? Could it be that the state is afraid of religion, and is protecting itself from truths about the rights of man which the state has no right to take away?

Is religious faith a leap into the dark or a leap into the light? That is a question that must be answered, because man's whole way of life depends on it. So let me propose one possible answer for reflection. I begin by pointing out that religious faith is only one type of faith. We live by faith not only in God but in one another. Each of us knows so little that we have to take on faith the knowledge and competence of others. For instance, when we read a book on science, we trust that the scientists and the author know what they are talking about. When we fly, we trust our lives to the competence of the pilot and flight engineers. By going to a doctor we express our faith in his medical expertise. When we buy food, we trust that no one is trying to poison us. In brief, without faith in one another we cannot live a human life.

Let us now turn to faith in God. What shall we say of *it*? First, how do we know God exists at all? St. Paul answers that briefly in his letter to the Romans (1:19 - 20), where he writes: "What can be known about God is plain . . . because God has

shown it. . . . Ever since the creation of the world his invisible nature, namely his eternal power and deity, has been clearly perceived by the things that have been made." In other words, we either admit God made the cosmos, or we have *no explanation at all!* Belief is more reasonable than unbelief.

But how do we know that God has spoken to man? We know it through the prophets, and through the miracles which go on to this day. Above all, we know it through the life, resurrection, and miracles of Jesus. By His miracles and by His life, which is a miracle of goodness, we know God spoke through Him. Perhaps I should add that, above all, we know God has spoken because we experience Him in our lives!

If it is right to believe good men, how much more reasonable it is to believe God, as St. John indicates in his first letter. If we do not believe in God, the state will lead us to believe it can take away our God-given rights.

Far from being foolish or weak, "this is the victory that overcomes the world, our faith" (1 Jn. 5:4).

12. Sight Without Eyes

Do you appreciate the greatness of the gift of faith? Do you know what wonderful vision it gives you?

An ancient Greek tradition tells us that the great poet Homer was blind. Now anyone who has read Homer's works knows that Homer saw more deeply into things than most men with the gift of sight. Yet the Gospels tell us of a blind man named Bartimaeus who had more wonderful vision than Homer.

We read about Bartimaeus in the tenth chapter of Mark. Blind Bartimaeus was sitting by the roadside when he heard a commotion and knew that a crowd was approaching. Somebody told Bartimaeus that Jesus was in the crowd. That was enough for Bartimaeus. He raised his voice and shouted: "Jesus, Son of David, have mercy on me!" Many of the people scolded Bartimaeus and told him to keep quiet. But he only shouted the louder.

Now why did people try to shut him up? I suggest it was because, though they could see Jesus with their own eyes, they did not really believe in Him. They did not think Jesus could or would do anything for this noisy nuisance, Bartimaeus. I think their thought ran like this: "Jesus is a nice man, probably even a holy man, but let's not get excited about Him, or really believe He can work those miracles which some simpletons claim He has been working. Let's keep religion from getting troublesome and stirring up gullible fools."

But Bartimaeus, who could not see Jesus, saw more in Him than they did. In front of all those people he was willing to cry out his faith and hope. Let us think about that for a moment: If Bartimaeus's faith proved unjustified, he would certainly be taken for a fool. But Bartimaeus knew he was right, and he shouted: "Jesus, Son of David, have mercy on me!" And Jesus said: "Go your way; your faith has made you well." And Bartimaeus looked up into the sun and saw the face of Jesus Christ.

But let us not get so carried away by the gift of sight restored that we overlook the greater gift Bartimaeus had received. Before ever his bodily eyes were opened he had been given that marvelous sight within, that sight that needs no bodily eyes, which we call faith. With his bodily eyes he could see what God had made, but with his inner eyes he could see by faith the God who made it.

Astronomers have telescopes and can see into the depths of space, so that the Indians call them "the men with the long eyes." But Bartimaeus had the telescope of faith and without eyes he could look right into the Heart of Jesus, the Heart of God, and his own heart could say to God: "I trust you, I love you, I know You care for me. Then take care of me! Heal me!" And Jesus did.

Blind Bartimaeus's experience suggests that we too ought to close our eyes and reflect on God and pray to Him. Closing our bodily eyes can help us open further the eyes of our faith. Then maybe we will see as deeply into the Heart of Jesus as Bartimaeus did.

13. The Pattern of Our Love

Do we need a pattern to know how to love rightly? What is the norm for love?

Once I asked a class of children this question: "Where did Sir Isaac Newton discover the law of gravity?" They gave various answers, but not one said, "In the apple he saw falling. The apple knew how to fall because the law of gravity was part of its nature."

The point of this example is that God wrote the laws of nature in things long before men wrote them in books. And long before God wrote the Ten Commandments on two stone tablets He wrote them into the heart of man. The only reason He had to write them on tablets is that by sin Adam and Eve darkened the human mind so that man could no longer read the law of love imprinted in his heart.

Later on, when God gave the Jews the stone tablets, they were rightly proud that they knew the way of life. But sadly, the commandments which lit up their minds did not much warm their hearts. Who wants to march through life behind two cold stone tablets?

Thus it was that our Father in heaven took pity on us and sent His Divine Son to become a man. Jesus is the new Adam. Jesus is God who also became man, a man without sin. His mind was not darkened, and so He could read the law of love written into His human flesh and blood, and live it to the full. And so He is the pattern of our love. We do not march through

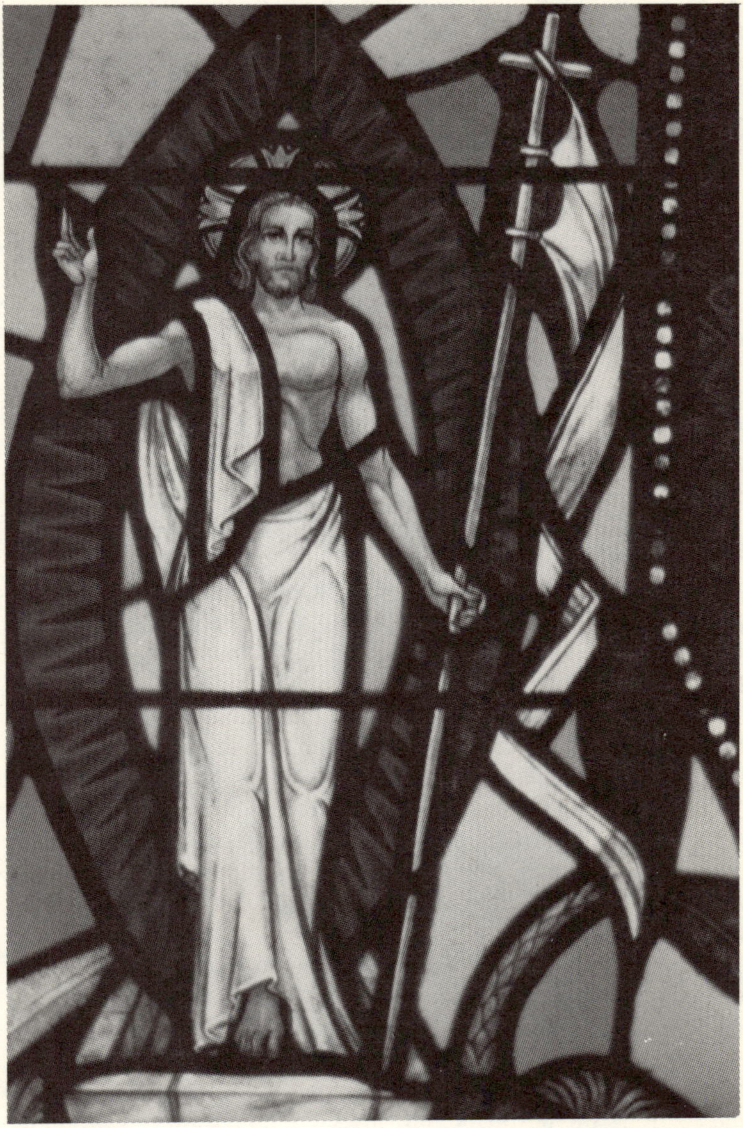

life in the wake of two stone tablets. We walk in the footsteps of Christ.

When some Christians are told they must be like Jesus, they object: "Oh, but He was God." In saying this, they obscure the whole meaning of the Incarnation, by which Jesus became as human as any of us. They also fail to understand Jesus when He says: "I am the way, and the truth, and the life" (Jn. 14:6).

If we are faithful Christians, we keep the humanity of Jesus ever before our eyes. We are called Christians because we are "other Christs." We not only follow Jesus, we enter into union with Him so that we become one mind and heart with Him. This union is not a matter of mere imitation either. It is something mysterious Jesus makes possible by giving us rebirth in baptism, and by entering into us through the Eucharist, and by sharing His Holy Spirit with us, as He promised at the Last Supper.

The Holy Spirit is Jesus' own guiding Love given to us. We can be sensitive to the Spirit only if we constantly "watch and pray," and then act with peace and joy, in accord with God's revelation and His teaching Church. If we act thus, we can be sure we are acting in the love of Jesus and in our own true love.

St. Paul gives a beautiful description and praise of love in his first letter to the Corinthians. I would like to quote part of that passage, but since Jesus is the pattern of our love, I will substitute His Name for the word "love": "Jesus is not arrogant or boastful. . . . Jesus does not insist on His own way; Jesus is not irritable or resentful; Jesus does not rejoice at wrong, but rejoices in the right. Jesus bears all things . . . endures all things" (1 Cor. 13:4 - 7).

This is Jesus, the pattern of our love. As we contemplate Jesus, let us hear as addressed to us those words He once spoke to another man: "Go and do likewise."

14. No Devotion for Losers

Is devotion to the Sacred Heart meant to console Christ for His failure to win the world's love? Is it a devotion of defeat or of victory?

We seldom think of it, but our devotion to Christ and His Sacred Heart can, like all things human, become defective and stand in need of correction. The one defect I propose that we examine ourselves on is this: Do we behave as though Jesus had lost His campaign for the world's love, so that all we can do is offer Him our love as a kind of consolation prize? This attitude may be well-meaning, but it is contrary to God's revelation. I call it the defeat syndrome.

This defeat syndrome is a trap easy to fall into. It seems to go all the way back to the Apostle Thomas. When Thomas saw Jesus going to defeat and death in Jerusalem, he exhorted the other Apostles: "Let us also go, that we may die with him" (Jn. 11:16). Yet later on, when told of Jesus' victory over death, he refused to believe. In other words, Thomas loved Jesus enough to be a loser with Him, but by reason of weak faith he was not ready to be a winner with Him!

Some friends of Jesus act like Thomas today. They look at the world's sad state, and they offer Jesus a sad love in His defeat — as they judge it! But this defeat syndrome won't square with the teaching of Jesus. At the Last Supper, facing betrayal on the spot and death the next day, Jesus said: "Be of good cheer, I have overcome the world" (Jn. 16:33). The next day He won victory over men's hatred by dying for love of them. Three days later He won victory over death itself. For two thousands years since He has been driving back the forces of sin and planting love. To get an idea of the horror of a world without Christ, picture it without its millions of Christian churches, schools, hospitals, dedicated priests, Sisters, and lay people.

No, devotion to the Sacred Heart is not for losers but for winners. It is for people who want to swell the victory of Christ and share it. To offer Christ our love is to change defeat to victory not for Him but for us, because "to serve him is to reign."

When Jesus appeared to St. Margaret Mary He did complain of a lack of love and asked for love. But He also claimed ultimate victory, for He showed her not only His Heart crushed by sin but His Heart glorious in triumph and He prophesied: "I shall reign." Therefore, devotion to the Sacred Heart calls us both to offer the reparation of sorrow for our lack of love, and to look forward in joy to the day Christ will complete His work among men so that countless numbers will be saved and will love Him as they ought (cf. Rev. 7:9).

If we return to St. Thomas, we recall that Jesus gave him the chance to see His risen body, and to see that His pierced Heart was once again full of life and joy. At once Thomas renounced the defeat syndrome. He traveled all the way to India proclaiming the Good News of Christ's victory.

In a world so full of defeatists and quitters, it is only right that lovers of the Heart of Jesus show the hope and the joy and the zeal of winners because their inheritance is not defeat but victory — the victory of Christ, who has overcome the world, and who says in promise to each one who fights faithfully to the end, "I will grant him to sit with me on my throne" (Rev. 3:21).

15. The Easter Christ in Our Lives

What is the meaning of Jesus' resurrection? Does it affect us now, or only in the future?

Jesus Christ has risen from the dead, and we rejoice for His sake, but He also wants us to rejoice for our own sakes. One day He will raise us too from the dead.

What I propose that we consider here is the present effect of Jesus' resurrection: Does it have any meaning for us right away? Is it only a promise, or does it change our lives here and now?

To answer that question I examined the Scriptures to find out what immediate effects the resurrection of Jesus had on His followers. I found that the Easter Jesus brought each of them what each needed most at the time.

To the women who went in tears to anoint His dead body Jesus gave the joy of His living presence, a joy no man could take away. To lonely Mary Magdalene, who had more love for Him than understanding of His real identity, He brought the joy of hearing her name spoken with that innocent love which He alone had given her, and in that love she recognized her risen Lord.

To the Twelve chosen to be witnesses to the world He came through solid walls, and they saw Him; He invited them to touch Him, talk with Him, and feed Him — and thus gather the evidence they most needed to tell all the world of His resurrection. And He breathed on them — they felt His living breath — and He gave them the power to forgive sin, which is power to bring peace to the world.

To the tottering faith of St. Thomas He brought the evidence of His wounded heart and wounded hands and living body — evidence upon which Thomas built an unshakeable belief in both His risen humanity and His eternal Divinity. To the two despairing travelers on the road to Emmaus He brought at twilight the rising sun of a hope that would never set. To Saul of Tarsus he brought blazing light that exposed his blind and twisted zeal, and lit up his heart with a fire which has illumined the world ever since.

These first activities of the risen Jesus make it clear that He is the great Consoler. The Easter Jesus comes to each of us to bring us what we need most now. He did not die to leave us but to rise from the dead transformed so as to be with us more than ever.

We do not need to await the Second Coming of Jesus to profit by His resurrection. The risen Jesus communicates now with us each time we turn to Him in prayer. In the events of our lives, Jesus the Lord of history is coming to us just as He came unrecognized to Mary Magdalene — unrecognized until she penetrated to His identity by recognizing His love.

Above all, the risen Jesus comes to each of us personally in the Eucharist. He Himself virtually called the Eucharist the Sacrament of Resurrection. He said: "Truly, truly, I say to you, unless you eat the flesh of the Son of man and drink his blood, you have no life in you; he who eats my flesh and drinks my blood has eternal life, and I will raise him up at the last day" (Jn. 6:52 - 54). Notice that Jesus is saying He pours eternal life into us now. Holy Communion is for the present as well as for the future. It is spiritual food, and like bodily food it gives nourishment, pleasure, growth, and healing. We may be sure that each time we receive Holy Communion Jesus our risen Consoler brings us what we need most now. Each time we go to Holy Communion, we are saying: Easter in me now, Lord Jesus!

16. This Is to Know Jesus

Just what is Devotion to the Sacred Heart of Jesus? Would it help you to hear one priest give personal witness to his experience of Jesus?

From the beginning the men and women who knew Jesus personally told others about Him so they too could believe. Permit me to continue that ancient tradition by witnessing to my personal experience of Jesus and of the love of His heart.

It was life in the Catholic Church which introduced me to Jesus, that mysterious "Son of Man." Jesus is mysterious — and yet I feel I know Him better than I know any other person.

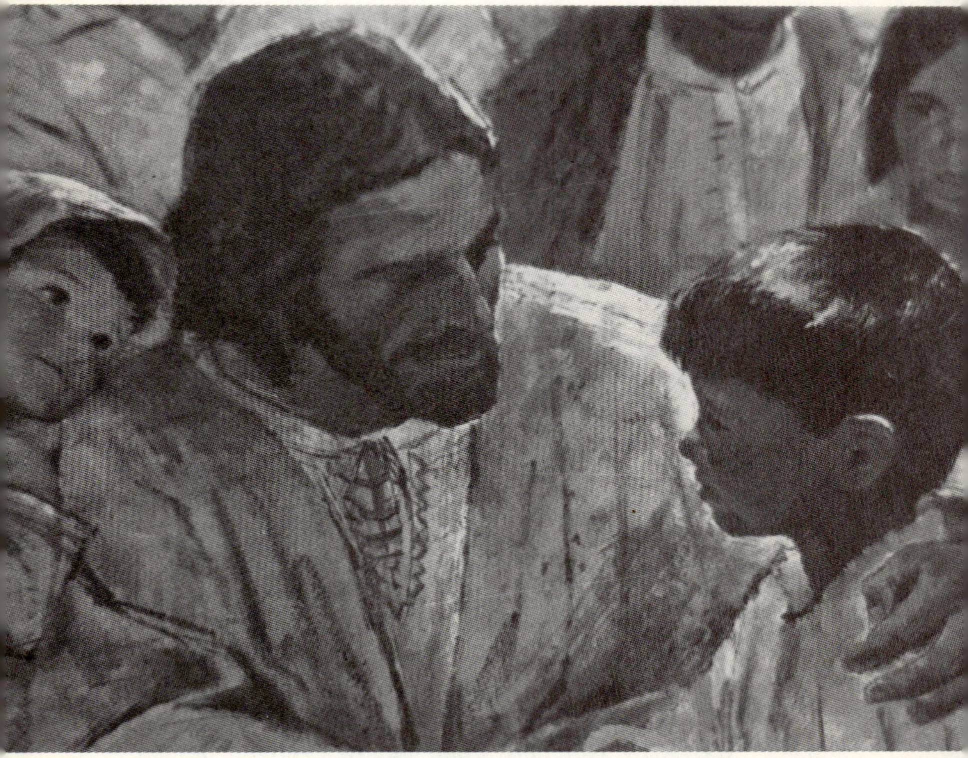

I know Jesus through many years of learning what the Church teaches about Him. I know Him through many years of talking to Him in prayer. I know Jesus through offering Him daily in the Mass and worshiping Him with my fellow believers, and receiving Him in the Eucharist, and meditating on Him in the Scriptures, and meeting Him in the Spirit. I know Him through feeling His personal influence changing me into His likeness as I take on His work and serve His people and walk the way of the cross with Him. I know Him through His friends, who show me His love and concern. And thus I have come to that kind of deep fellowship with Jesus which makes us say of another that we have a heart-to-heart relationship with him.

I have affection for Jesus in His real inner self, and a sense of His like affection for me. I find that Jesus' love for me has fostered in me a healthy love for myself, and it has led to a greater love of others and a healthier love of life.

My experience of Jesus is the experience of salvation. Without Jesus, life to me is a sinful stretch of consciousness beginning nowhere and leading nowhere. With Jesus, my life is meaningful, innocent, and rescued from death forever. But Jesus does not make my life easy; He only makes it happy. He gives me the light and the power to live as my heart challenges me to, so that like Him I hope to go my way in strength and "leave the earth a man."

Jesus makes religion my joy by helping me to know God intimately and to trust in Him profoundly. Jesus helps me to know God in that Jesus is "God suited to our sight"; for in Jesus I meet God as both one of us and the One beyond us, just as Paul describes it when he writes of Jesus: "Though he was in the form of God . . . he emptied himself . . . being born in the likeness of men" (Phil. 2:6 - 7). I find Jesus' heart one with my heart in tasting the joys of life, grieving at its sorrows, pounding with its fears, and melting with its loves. Such oneness with Jesus makes me esteem life as worthwhile even in moments when without Jesus I would despair. Jesus makes me trust God profoundly, for the God who gave us His Son and the God who is the Son given to us must then be willing to give us everything that is really good for us, as the common sense of St. Paul makes evident: "He who did not spare his own Son, but gave him up for us all, will he not also give us all things with him?" (Rom. 8:32).

I love Jesus with a love I can give to no mere human being. My love for Jesus is therefore mysterious, with something divine about it, because I have been reborn of God. St. Peter wrote: "Your rebirth has come . . . from an indestructible seed through the living and enduring word of God" (1 Peter 1:23 NAT).

What Jesus has become for me He is meant to be for all. "Come to me," He says, "all who labor and are heavy laden, and I will give you rest. Take my yoke upon you and learn from me, for I am gentle and lowly in heart, and you will find rest for your souls" (Mt. 11:28 - 29).

17. The Fourth of July and the Mass

What does the celebration of the Mass have in common with the celebration of our country's founding? Can a comparison of the Mass and the Fourth of July help us to appreciate both better?

There is a marked similarity between the celebration of the Fourth of July and the celebration of the Mass. The Fourth of July celebrates the birth of our nation. The Mass celebrates the Lord's death and resurrection which gave birth to the people of God.

The Fourth of July commemorates the signing of the Declaration of Independence; but it also calls to mind the many

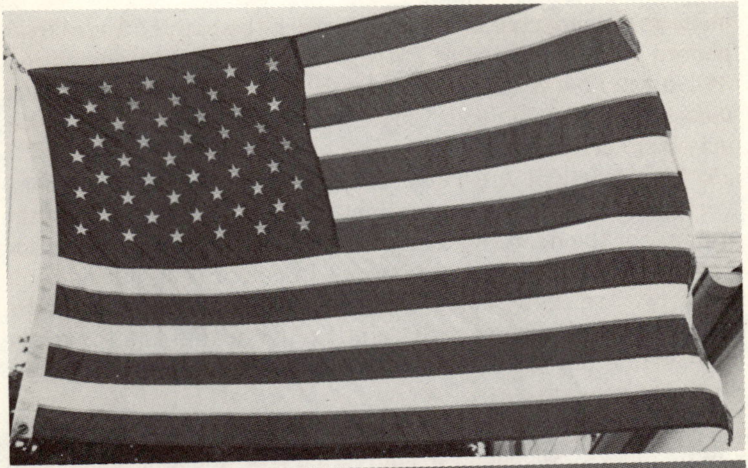

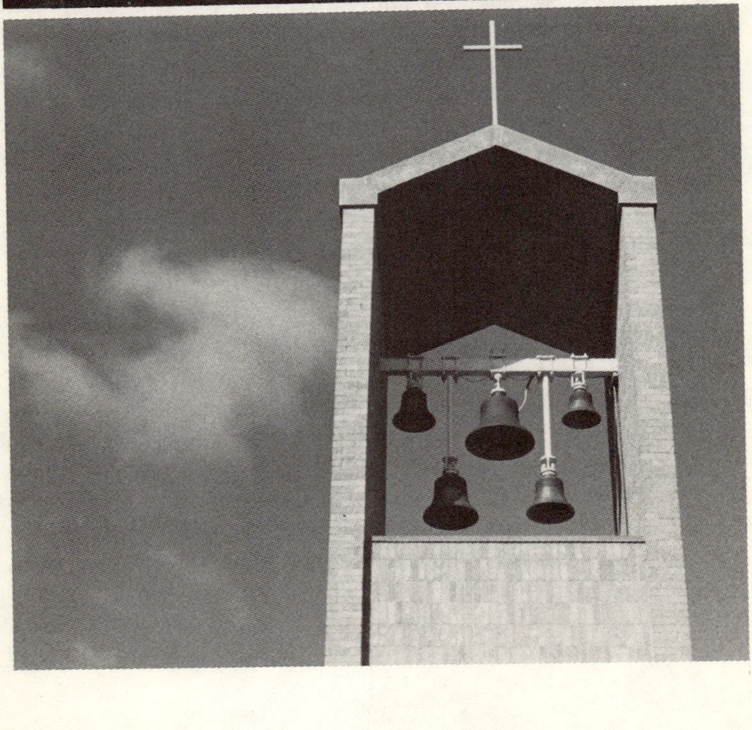

noble men who gave this nation birth in the bath of their blood, poured out in the spirit of Patrick Henry, who cried in passion, "Give me liberty or give me death!" The people of God were born in the blood of Jesus Christ whose passionate love won liberty from death itself.

The Fourth of July celebrates the two-hundredth-plus anniversary of the birth of our nation. We celebrate the birth of the living, not the dead. Who celebrates ancient Babylon, a nation known only to the dust of history? In celebrating our nation's birth, we are really celebrating also the years since its birth, the years of victory over dissolution and death. And so we are celebrating ourselves, for we are that new nation as it exists today.

The celebration of the Mass is approaching its bimillennium, the two-thousandth anniversary of the Church's birth through Christ's victory over sin and death. In this case too, we are not merely celebrating a memory — we are celebrating the risen life of Jesus, which goes on even now. More, we are celebrating ourselves in Him, for His victory over death spreads to us through Mass and Communion. Jesus Himself taught this when He said: "He who feeds on my flesh and drinks my blood has eternal life, and I will raise him up on the last day" (Jn. 6:54 NAT). Just as we the citizens continue the life of our nation, we the members of Christ continue His life in the world, for we are His mystical body.

The Fourth of July celebrates that day of two hundred-plus years ago when brave men and bold signed the Declaration of Independence in a council chamber in Philadelphia — but before they begot the nation we have inherited they still had to go forth and create in fact what they had only created on paper that day. We too, when we gather together as God's people to celebrate Christ's victory over selfishness and death, must then go forth from the chamber of the Mass into the world to carry there the service of love that will turn the world into the kingdom of God, a kingdom whose Declaration of Independence from sin and death was signed in the blood of Christ on the hill of Calvary. To serve that kingdom we too must be "eager for noble deeds" (Tit. 2:14).

Two centuries ago "our fathers brought forth on this continent a new nation, conceived in liberty, and dedicated to the proposition that all men are created equal." Certain self-styled "superior" persons scorn this proposition — and so the fight for the survival of our nation goes on.

Similarly, we the people of God fight daily on behalf of the embattled truths revealed by Jesus Christ — the truths of faith upon which we take our stand.

When we celebrate a friend's birthday we spiritedly wish him many more years of happiness. In the same spirit, let us offer the following prayer: O Lord, we pray that we may so live as citizens of our country that we may hand on our nation intact to our children and our children's children. And as members of Christ's true Church may we so live that we faithfully hand on the salvation entrusted to us, and pass through death to resurrection to join Jesus face to face in our true homeland. Amen.

18. The Catholic and the Common Good

What does the Catholic, in common with all other citizens, owe to his country? What special service does he owe his country precisely because he is Catholic?

Some two centuries ago our nation was founded on a common vision of the common good plus a readiness to sacrifice for that common good. The annual Fourth of July celebration of our nation's founding invites us to reflect on our forefathers' vision of the common good, which we have inherited.

One of the greatest dangers for a democracy is that individuals and cliques will spurn the common good and scheme and shout for their own selfish interests. When this begins — and it has begun — a nation is on the decline.

Common sense calls us to meditate on the common good and to vow to uphold it for love of God and country.

What is the common good? What good do all of us as a nation have in common? That question is answered by the Preamble of the Constitution of the United States: "We the people of the United States, in Order to form a more perfect Union, establish Justice, insure domestic Tranquility, provide for the common defence, promote the general Welfare, and secure the Blessings of Liberty to ourselves and our Posterity, do ordain and establish this CONSTITUTION for the United States of America."

This is the common good, and we Catholics, in league with all our fellow countrymen, have the job of promoting it as our first patriotic duty.

Second, we Catholics have the special duty of showing our countrymen a deep reverence for legitimate authority. The Church is famed for inculcating obedience and for teaching that all right authority is from God and all obedience is for God, whether to bishops or to governors. This is the revelation. St. Peter writes: "Be subject for the Lord's sake to every human institution..." (1 Peter 2:13).

Third, Catholics together with all believers have the duty of preserving the common good by rejecting all godless acts of authority. The recent decision of the Supreme Court claiming abortion a right of citizens flies in the face of the law of God and the law of nations — Thou shalt not kill — and can only be outrightly rejected and condemned, and I reject and condemn it. In the words of St. Peter to *his* nation: "Judge for yourselves whether it is right in God's sight for us to obey you rather than God" (Acts 4:19 NAT).

Finally, about freedom: It is a venerable American battle cry that "Taxation without representation is tyranny." But that is only one kind of tyranny. Look at the tyranny in education today. Our government pretends to uphold our God-given right to educate our children as we see fit. What it actually does is force every citizen to support the public schools — thus stripping citizens of the money they need to educate their children in their own way. Taxation that destroys freedom of education is tyranny. There are democracies which do not practice this tyranny. They shame us and outshine our vaunted freedom. To fight this tyranny over our freedom is not only our right — it is our duty to God and our patriotic duty in the service of the common good. All believers and all who love God — just as all who love freedom — must, in the words of a fellow-countryman, "hang together or we will all hang separately."

Blind selfishness threatens the common good today. In God's name let us purify our hearts and our country by the way we live and seek the good of all. This is to be both a man of God and a patriot. By promoting the good of all we will find God and one another — and that is the good of each of us.

19. Friends of the Wedding

When we think of ways to make a marriage a success, do we think too much of the wedding couple and what they must do? Should we talk more of what others must do — what we must do?

I recently made a long trip to meet with relatives and friends in a distant city. As we met together, I asked myself reflectively, "Why have we come here? Why have we all gone to this considerable trouble?" And the answer popped into my head readily enough: Obviously, it is the wedding that brought us. My nephew John invited me to his wedding, and this is the city of his bride." But to that facile answer I responded: "No, a love has brought us here — John's and Vikki's love. Why has it brought us? To honor it, to enjoy it, to serve and support it on their wedding day. Their love has overflowed. We have enjoyed it, and reflected it back upon them and made it grow and burst into fire and flame."

What began to appear to me more clearly than ever before is this, that a wedding is not an affair of two. No couple is an island.

We speak readily of the married couple's joys, and of their mutual rights and obligations, but how often do we remember that marriage is a mystery in which we too — the relatives and friends of the wedding — have our obligations and our rights? We have the obligation to nurture the union of the wedding couple by whatever we have of virtue and possessions. We have the obligation to keep our defects from injuring their union.

We have the right to expect of them that they will be faithful to their love and bring us happiness by their happiness. Their happiness is not theirs alone. Their married love involves them in two great mysteries. The first is the mystery of humanity. A man who marries one woman draws closer to all women and all humanity. A woman who marries one man draws closer to all men and all humanity. Even on the day of their wedding their love is overflowing and enriching others, as we have often experienced. One day in the normal course of events it will overflow into lifegiving — and their parents will see their gift of life surging into the future — given again!

The second mystery in which their marriage involves them is the mystery of Christ. St. Paul says of the marriage union: "This is a great mystery; I mean that it refers to Christ and the Church" (Eph. 5:32). The wedding couple's faithful perpetual love bodies forth Christ's love for us and makes us trust more in the fidelity of His love for us — we who are His body. What then if the married couple are not faithful to their love? Their unfaithfulness would wound our faith and therefore our salvation.

Love is always of two, but it is never of two alone. The married couple has need of the friends of the wedding, and the friends have need of them.

PART B

20. The Enigma of God

Why does God claim to give us His Son, yet take our own sons and daughters in untimely deaths? Why do events seem to contradict God's claim that He loves us?

We are all beset by experiences that war against our faith in God and His love. Faith portrays one set of divine actions. Experience gives us a contrasting set. Faith says that God loves us so much He gives us His only Son. Experience says He takes our own sons and daughters in untimely deaths, and He takes our wives and husbands, brothers and sisters, fathers and mothers.

The Bible tells of the care with which God prepared for the coming of His Son ages ahead of time, and experience tells us of the carelessness with which He seems to cut off the life and health of our loved ones and ourselves. Why? One woman of faith told me how this dilemma was solved for her. Her husband died. She was shattered. One day she was washing up in the bathroom and she heard a voice. It said: "I never make a mistake."

She was astounded. The words were repeated: "I never make a mistake." She fell on her knees. For the third time she heard the words: "I never make a mistake." From then on she was convinced of the providence of God. God was say-

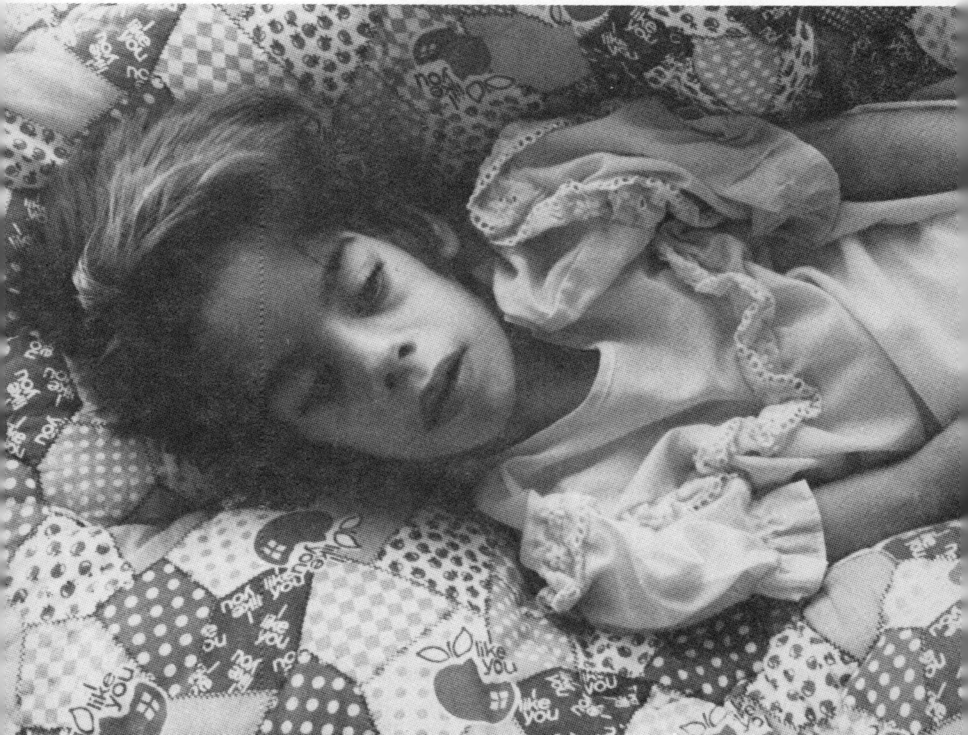
like you

ing: "My providence never fails you. It is the same as my care for Jesus."

When we think of it, we realize that Jesus too died an untimely death, with Joseph already dead, leaving Mary a widow bereaved of her only Son. Then this mystery of God's contradictory love applies to Jesus too. But that only broadens the mystery, it does not explain it. What does explain it?

I think the enigma of God is solved if we give up the self-centered view that God is a kind of Almighty Servant whose job it is to arrange things as we would like; arrange things for our human love affairs, and He must stay out of them. The enigma is solved if we accept the following proposition: The most important love affair in creation is that between God and each human soul. That relationship is more important than all else. It is more important than that between husband and wife, parents and children, brothers and sisters.

Since the love affair between God and each soul comes first, and since God is the Lord of history, He arranges life and death and everything else according to the divine love affair between Him and each soul. If we take this view we can compare life to a large room in which the most beautiful and conspicuous piece of furniture is arranged first, and the other pieces are suited to it. God is that beautiful piece.

Our life becomes a garden where God walks — and plucks each piece of fruit when it is ripe. The tree does not say, *Why do you pluck my fruit?* For the fruit does not belong to the tree but to the gardener.

And so even if we lose a loved one through his untimely death we can learn to say what the Book of Wisdom says: "He who pleased God was loved; he who lived among sinners was transported — snatched away lest wickedness pervert his mind" (4:10 - 11 NAT) — snatched up to immortality.

If we take this view of life, we will find that the enigma of God is simply a mystery of undeserved love poured out on each one of us.

21. Trailblazer of the Sacred Heart Devotion

What is genuine devotion to the Heart of Jesus? Is there anyone whose life exemplifies true devotion to the Sacred Heart?

Our Lord has given each of us a most profound, personal, and intimate invitation to know Him: "Come to me, all you who labor and are heavy laden, and I will give you rest. Take my yoke upon you, and learn from me: for I am gentle and lowly in heart, and you will find rest for your souls" (Mt. 11:28 - 29). If we recognize in these words an invitation to devotion to the Heart of Jesus, we recognize at once that devotion to His Heart is not the mere sentimentality some people think it is.

Pius XII wrote an Encyclical on Devotion to the Sacred Heart. In it he said: "This devotion is nothing else than devotion to the human and divine love of the Incarnate Word and to the love which the heavenly Father and the Holy Spirit have for sinful men." This devotion, he went on, leads us "to fulfill more fervently the principal duties of the Catholic faith, namely the obligations of love and expiation." It is, therefore, he wrote, "the perfect profession of the Christian religion."

The devotion of a dog for a man sheds light on what devotion to Jesus should be. A dog can associate with a man because a man is a bodily creature of five senses like itself. It can become attached to a man who is its master because its master provides food and shelter. But more mysteriously it offers a kind of worship to a man because a man is more than itself.

Similarly, we love the God-man not only because He became a man — became like us — but because in His Divinity He forever remains more than us. He remains the Son of God, able to provide for us in life and death, time and eternity. As

He Himself said: "I am the resurrection and the life. . . . I go to prepare a place for you" (Jn. 11:25; 14:2).

In living the devotion to the Sacred Heart, there are two extremes to avoid. The one is to so emphasize the Divinity of Jesus that for all practical purposes we deny that He is human. The other extreme is to so emphasize His humanity that we lose faith in His Divinity.

There is one person who most perfectly escaped both of these extremes, and practiced perfect devotion to the Heart of Jesus. That person is His Mother, Mary. How could she fail to believe He is fully human when she felt His tiny body growing in her womb; when she held Him to her breast to nourish Him just like other babies; when she saw Him growing at her side; when she saw Him walk the earth a man; when she saw Him suffer, saw Him die on the cross with His own breast pierced? How could she fail to believe He was Divine when she heard the angel Gabriel say of Him: "He . . . will be called the Son of the Most High . . . and of His Kingdom there will be no end" (Luke 1:32 - 33)? And when she conceived Him without the help of a man? And she saw His miracles — saw Him risen and glorious and full of power?

And we in our turn can practice true devotion to the Heart of Jesus if we imitate Mary. By meditating on the mysteries of the life of Jesus as they are known to us from the Gospels, we can in a way, by the use of our imagination, share her experiences of Jesus; and by pondering those experiences we can like Mary come to know Him as true God and true Man, and come to a true and genuine devotion to His Sacred Heart.

22. The Love You Save May Be Your Own

Why do people destroy what they love most? What is the secret of safeguarding what we love?

Two teenage boys stood on a very high bridge. They had been drinking. They incited each other to jump into the water far, far below. One jumped — to his death! The other lived to suffer the horror of it.

A famous author long ago wrote the awful words: ". . . each man kills the thing he loves. . . ." These words apply to more than the two boys on the bridge. They apply to Adam and Eve, and to Cain and Abel. They apply to millions of married couples who with a river of words of bitterness and bickering kill the sweet love that had made them man and wife. They fit the millions of parents and children who have murdered the love for one another which was their gift from God. They apply to the innocence we slay by sin. With one thrust of the sword of sin we slay both the innocent body of Christ on the Cross and the lovely innocence of our own souls.

Why do we kill the things we love? Because we love them too little. We love too much every escape from suffering, so we lash out at whatever causes us a little pain — even if it is the beloved. We are too fond of illicit pleasure, and so we kill love and truth and integrity to get it. We are too attached to our own prestige, and so we cut down even those we love so that we may seem to stand taller than they. In all these ways we fail to love, and so we kill the little love we have.

What can stop us from killing the things we love? Only one thing: a greater love. What is the way to that greater love? It is called The Way of the Cross. Take up a crucifix and study it. It is the Book of the Saints. The philosophers say: "Nothing awakens love like seeing yourself loved first." Look at the

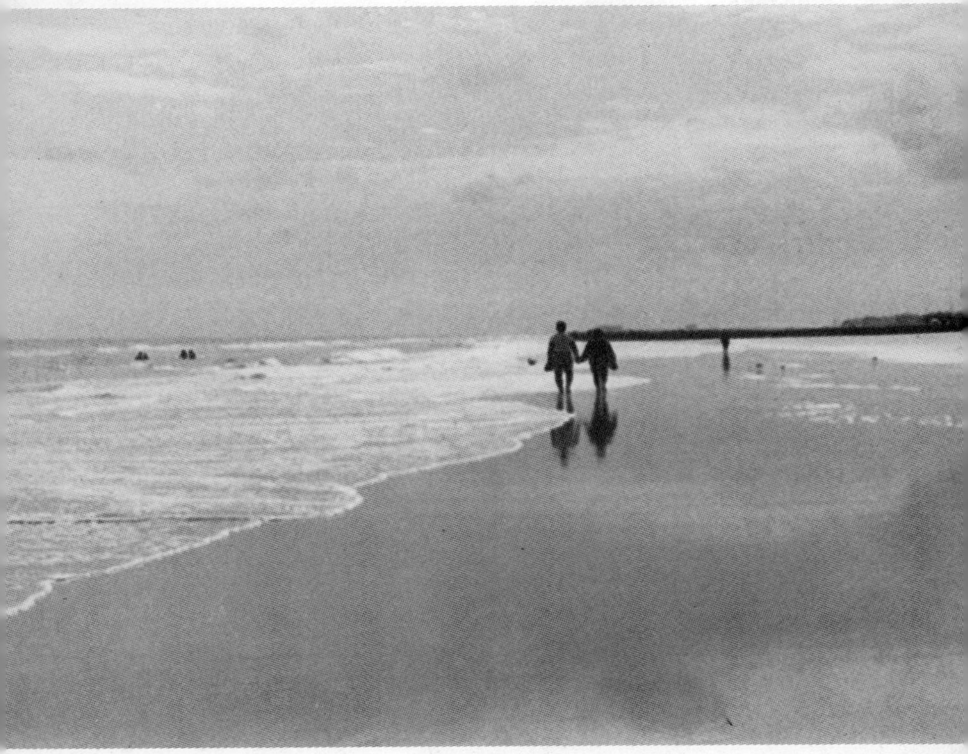

crucifix and say to Jesus: "You have loved me and delivered Yourself for me."

Ponder how the Innocent One is being punished for our sins. Nothing awakens compassionate love like seeing Innocence suffer. Say to the Crucified: "These wounds, my Lord, Thou makes Thine. / Share them with me, for they are mine."

Make the Stations of the Cross, and at each station say the self-same words: "Lord Jesus, take me with You."

If we will not willingly shoulder our share of suffering we will continue to kill the things we love. Jesus said that "unless a grain of wheat falls into the earth and dies, it remains alone" (Jn. 12:24).

If we refuse to shoulder our cross, we will be like the nobleman sitting in the tavern carousing with his friends. There is a commotion outdoors, and one friend looks up and cries to the nobleman: "Isn't that the king's son? Isn't that your brother? Why is he in chains?" And the nobleman answers: "Yes, it is my brother. I was condemned to death, and he offered to die in my place. But it's a sad story. Let's play cards." And his friends stare at him in horror.

Each of us has his choice: to be the ignoble nobleman, or Simon of Cyrene who carried the cross with Jesus.

23. Sweet Mystery of Life

Have you ever really identified a purpose in life? Have you ever drawn up a strategy to make that purpose real in your life?

Someone has observed that parents can know their children are grown up when they stop asking where they come from and refuse to tell where they are going! An even better sign of maturity is when they stop asking where they come from and start asking where they are going — that is, when they look to the meaning and purpose of life.

To be mature, each of us has to ask the question: What am I seeking? A pagan poet answered: "A jug of Wine, a Loaf of Bread — and Thou. . . ." And he was right as far as he went. Our basic needs are food and companionship.

But all except the atheist go further than the pagan poet and insist that the Thou for which I long is not simply my mate, my mother, or my brother, but my God. He is the first Being and the source of all being, and my heart longs to return to Him.

Our thoughts may agree with this, but do our lives? What are we seeking? The clasp of a loving hand? The look of eyes adoring? The union of flesh with flesh? The security of an escalating bank account? Or perhaps the prestige of success? The pride of intellectual achievement? Or a home, a family, an hour in the sun before the decline into the shadows?

Jesus Christ told us what we ought to put first not only in thought but in deed. Seek first the kingdom of God, He said, and our other needs will be met too.

St. Ignatius of Loyola not only put God first in his own life, but he drew up a strategy to help us keep Him first in our lives on a day-to-day basis. He called this strategy the "Principle and Foundation." In it he said that, since God created all of us to return to Him by the right use of everything created, we should want to possess only what He wants for us. Therefore, we should not want wealth more than poverty, if we begin to see that for us personally poverty helps us to get to God more than riches do. And under like circumstances, we should not want health more than sickness, honor more than dishonor, or a long life more than a short one. We should want only what helps us most to praise, reverence and serve God, and thus enter into resurrection with Jesus Christ.

Once a wealthy man read the Principle and Foundation, and exclaimed to me: "You mean I shouldn't care if I lose all my wealth!" I said he should not, if it happened through God's will and not through his own fault. I reminded him that as a religious, I myself deliberately took a vow of poverty to be like Christ, poor, as He and the Church called me in my heart to do.

What we should be seeking is to live in the likeness of Christ and to leave the earth a saint. All who do this have solved the mystery of life and found that it is sweet.

24. Confession Is Too Easy

Why do Catholics make so little use of the sacrament of reconciliation? Could it be that it is too easy?

Once when I was working as a chaplain in a hospital, a non-Catholic man asked to speak with me. He had done something terrible. He wanted to get it off his chest. He knew that I could not give him sacramental absolution, but he told me what he had done anyway. I was able to assure him God would forgive him because he was sorry and repentant. But how much more I am able to do for a Catholic! By the power God and the Church gave me through ordination, I am able to say to the Catholic who confesses his sins with sorrow: "Through the ministry of the Church may God give you pardon and peace, and I absolve you from your sins in the Name of the Father, and of the Son, and of the Holy Spirit." This power goes back to the evening of the first Easter when Jesus came to His disciples and said to them "Peace be with you." Then He breathed on them and added: "Receive the Holy Spirit. If you forgive the sins of any, they are forgiven; if you retain the sins of any, they are retained" (Jn. 20:19, 23).

One psychiatrist, not himself a Catholic, reportedly told a Catholic bishop that if all religions required confession, it would put psychiatrists out of business. At any rate, it would certainly make fewer necessary. One priest went to a psychiatrist and was told: "Father, I can't take your money. You don't need a psychiatrist. You need to go to confession!" His problem was not disorder in his psyche, but unfaithfulness to his God.

The great psychiatrist Carl Jung wrote: "Confessions to one's secret self are almost useless; to another, much more promising." Long before Jung knew this, Jesus Christ knew it. That is one reason He gave us the rite of confession to a priest — to a fellow human being and sinner.

In the Book of Kings we read of Naaman the leper. He went to Elisha the miracle-worker to be cured. Elisha told him to wash seven times in the Jordan. Naaman went away angry. Here he had come all the way from Syria with its great rivers, expecting thunder, lightning and miracles, only to be told to wash in that mudhole of a Jordan! Fortunately, Naaman's wise servant pointed out to him that if Elisha had required something hard, he would have done it — so why not do this easy thing? Naaman was persuaded. He washed in the Jordan — and he came out with flesh as pure as a little child's.

Many Catholics fail to go to Jesus and His priests to be healed and freed of guilt. Why? Is it because confession is too difficult? Or because it is too easy? It is cheaper than a psychiatrist, less difficult than blackjacking one's conscience with further sins, and more simple than the come-on rituals of religious charlatans. What, then? Could it be that it's too simple — that, like Naaman, sinners don't believe in it because it's too easy? Perhaps God should apologize and say to us: I'm sorry I had to make it so easy, but I'm just that forgiving!"

The sacrament of confession is for peace and joy and celebration of forgiveness. Using it is the best way to say: "Thank you God, for making it so easy to receive Your forgiveness."

25. The Wonder of Christmas

Can we recover lost meaning in Christmas? Can we discover ever new meaning in Christmas?

Japan is not a Christian country, yet the Japanese have come to love Christmas. They have developed a passion for celebrating Christmas with gift-giving get-togethers. They have found a meaning in Christmas, but not *the* meaning. Many in our own land have lost the meaning of Christmas. Several years ago I saw a billboard with the message: *Put Christ back into Christmas!*

It is good for us to give one another gifts on Christmas, but it is bad if we forget their significance. It is bad if we forget we are moved to this generosity by God the Father who so loved us that on the first Christmas He gave us His only Son.

In the silent cold of the first Christmas, Mary brought Him forth like a rising Nile to bring a floodtime of joy to the world. Christmas is the day that God, who is everything we are not — Divine, glorious, immortal, powerful, serene — became everything we are — human, lowly, mortal, weak, tempted. He became everything we are except a sinner. He became everything we are without ceasing to be anything He is. He remained God while becoming man. Remaining one-hundred percent what He is, He became one-hundred percent what we are.

If He had not remained God's Son, what would it have profited us for Him to become our Son — a Son of man?

That is why we cannot understand Christmas if we consider it by itself alone. To understand Christmas we have to go to Easter. Easter is the day one of us — Christ Jesus — rose from the dead and became deathless.

To understand Christmas and Easter, we have to go to the Eucharist. The Eucharist is the mystery of the purpose of Christmas. It is the mystery in which God's Son, who became man through Mary and immortal through Easter, comes to

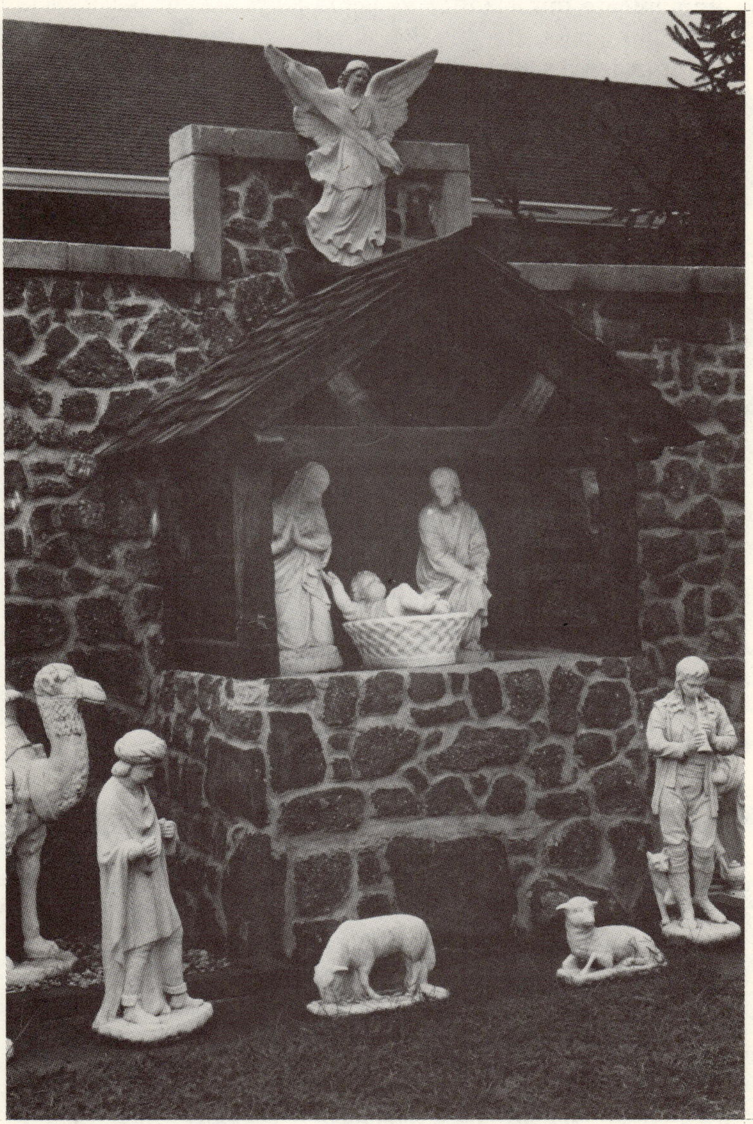

communicate immortality to us. Jesus revealed that through Holy Communion He, the Son of God, shares everlasting life with us and will raise us up on the last day.

Christmas is the day we recognize that "when the kindness and love of God our savior appeared, he saved us; not because of any righteous deeds we had done, but because of his mercy" (Tit. 3:4 - 5 NAT). It is the day we are even happy to be sinners since our need to be saved brings us such and so great a Savior.

Christmas is the day everyone wants to spend at home. That too is the work of God. It is the day God came home to us. It is the day we the human race first held God in our arms — in the arms of Mary. And so we call Jesus Emmanuel — which means God with us. Christmas is the day which gives us the sure hope of one day going home to God.

One year one little boy had such a fine Christmas he exclaimed: "Too bad every day can't be Christmas!" The surprising thing is, *it can!* The first Christmas, there was a birth. A birth brings into our families a child who comes to stay. That is what Christmas brought. And that is why Jesus promised: "I am with you always . . ." (Mt. 28:20). He is most fully with us in the Eucharist. Speaking about the Eucharist during Advent, 1977, Pope Paul VI said: "We must revive, and precisely by celebrating the great feast of Christmas, our faith in the mysterious and joyful Eucharistic presence among us. . . . Every day can be Christmas for us!" The wonder of Christmas is that it is the once and forever feast.

26. I Am a Sinner

Have you ever reflected on the danger involved in admitting you are a sinner? Have you ever realized the importance of the admission anyhow?

Why are we fragile and fallible mortals afraid to admit we are sinners? We are afraid because it is really dangerous! To

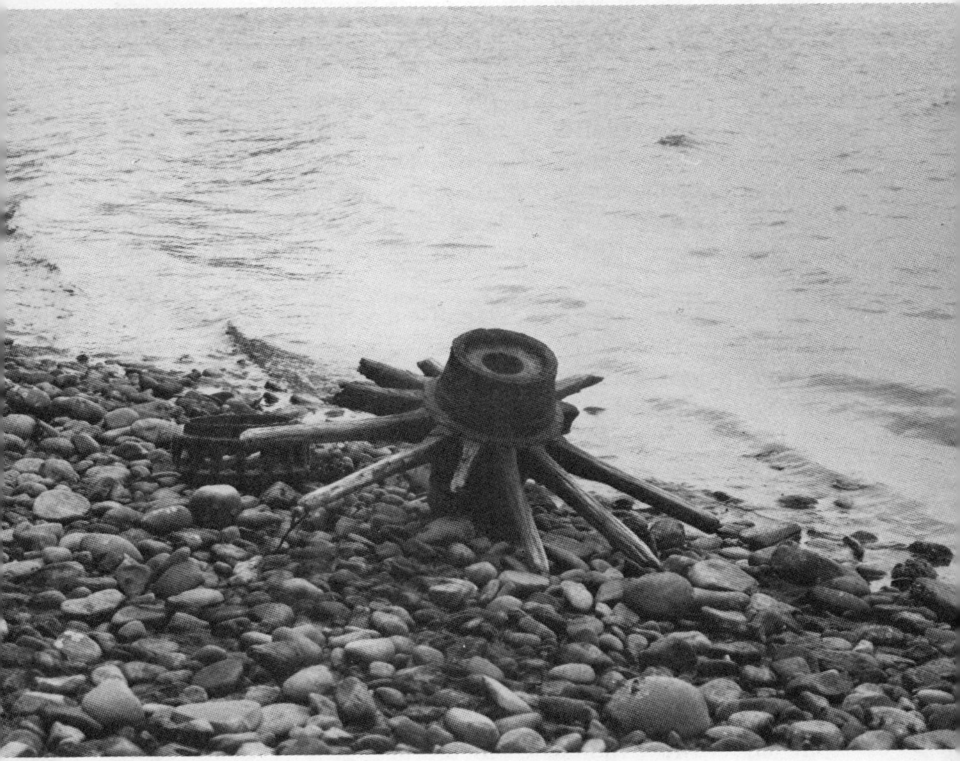

admit we are sinners is to confess we do evil. And if ever we should think of ourselves as evil, we might reject ourselves. Whereupon we might destroy ourselves.

And so, to protect ourselves against self-rejection and self-destruction, we mount an array of defenses against admitting our sins. Psychiatrists even have a name for this array. They call it the defense mechanism. It can take the form of repression, regression, aggression, and pretense.

Despite the danger of admitting our sinfulness, it is necessary. The reason for its necessity is that unless we face up to and experience ourselves as sinners in need of salvation, we cannot know Jesus. How can we experience the Savior except by experiencing ourselves as the saved ones?

In the parable of the Pharisee and the tax collector, Jesus teaches how blind we are to the need for our Savior until we know our own sinfulness. The Pharisee spent his prayer time thinking of other men's evil deeds and his good deeds. The tax collector spent his prayer time begging forgiveness for the evil deeds he so freely admitted doing. As a result he "went home from the temple justified but the other did not" (Lk. 18:14 NAT).

How can we gain knowledge of ourselves as sinners? The truth is that we can't — by ourselves. We cannot give ourselves this knowledge. Sin is an offense against God, and we cannot know He is offended unless He lets us know. We gain the knowledge that we are sinners by asking God to let us know what offends Him, by studying His Revelation, by listening to the Church, and by being sensitive to our offenses against one another. This latter point needs to be added because Christ taught that what we do to others we do to Him (cf. Mt. 25:45).

We can and ought to dispose ourselves to receive this knowledge of our sinfulness. First, we go back in prayer to the origin of human sinfulness. The reading of the opening chapters of the Book of Genesis reminds us that we are the offspring of sinners. Second, we ponder our own history of sin from our earliest memories to the present. We can keep it healthy if we never say: *How I have disappointed myself!* Instead we repeatedly say: "O God, be merciful to me, a sinner" (Lk. 18:13).

We should remember to go about this very cautiously, so as not to fall into self-hatred and self-rejection as Judas did. To this end it helps to remember: It is not the religious man who hates himself but the nonreligious man. The Bible teaches somewhere that it is the unrepentant sinner who hates his own soul. The examples of Judas and St. Peter confirm that. St. Peter denied Christ, but instead of despairing as Judas did he wept and sought forgiveness of the Lord he had offended.

Before examining our sinfulness, we ought to put ourselves in the presence of Jesus crucified and see how He loves us and delivers Himself up for us. Then we look up to the Father and see how He looks down upon us with love, wanting only to forgive us and create us as something more beautiful. We see how He sends the Son to lay down His life for us and to share His life with us. If we proceed in this way, no matter what sins we have to recall, we will never think we are rotten through and through. We are sinners, but God can put our sins from us as far as the East is from the West.

Our objective is to try to experience ourselves as helpless sinners saved up until now by our loving Father and His Divine Son. We need to feel shame at our unfaithfulness, and confusion at His goodness in still loving us. We need to sense the disordered impulses still alive in us, to weep for ourselves as Jesus counseled the daughters of Jerusalem. Then, in spirit, we rise up and go to our Father in prayer of repentance. We rise up and go to a priest and make a good confession.

And then, in peace and great joy, in self-acceptance and acceptance by God, we can say with St. Paul: "I have no righteousness of my own based on law, but that which is through faith in Jesus Christ, the righteousness of God that depends on faith" (cf. Phil. 3:8 f.).

27. How to Get What You Want from God

How can we influence God to give us what we want? What are the secrets of prayer of petition?

A boy visiting his grandfather's farm saw a beautiful horse and asked for it. "Boy," his grandfather said, "that foal is too costly to give away. But when *I* want anything, I pray for it. Why don't you pray for a horse?" "Grandfather," the boy replied, "since I don't always get what I pray for and you do, why don't you give me your horse, and *you* pray for one?"

This boy knew enough about the prayer of petition to keep us all honest. The Bible, too, tries to keep us honest and realistic about the prayer of petition. St. James writes: "You ask and do not receive, because you ask wrongly, to spend it on your passions" (James 4:3). In other words, God will not give us some things because we would misuse them. The man who is falling into sin because of misusing what he already has should ask for forgiveness, not for more possessions. God will not give a man what he prays for if it would make the man His enemy.

When Jesus was suffering in His agony, He asked the Father to save Him from the suffering, but to His prayer of petition He added this condition: "Nevertheless, not my will but thine be done" (Lk. 22:42).

The first rule, then, for getting what we want from God, is not to want what He does not want us to have. We must purify our intentions and our desires.

A parable will illustrate the second rule to be followed: A wealthy man had two sons. One asked his father for money to take a summer vacation in Europe, and got it. The other stayed home and moped around peevishly all summer. One day in a jealous rage he blurted out: "You gave my brother money for Europe, but not me!" "Son," his father replied, "you didn't ask me, and he did." The son exclaimed: "You knew I wanted to go! I hinted at it." His father answered: "You knew I want you to ask like a man when you want something. I have told you that repeatedly. To refuse to ask is to think you have it coming, or to think I would refuse you. Both attitudes insult me and ruin you. I will not spoil my children by humoring such attitudes." God is like that father. He wants us to ask for what we need, and not to take things for granted. Jesus said: "Ask and it will be given you" (Lk. 11:9). He taught us to pray even for our daily bread. And St. James adds: "You do not have because you do not ask" (James 4:2).

Our second rule for getting what we want from God is: *Be sure to ask for it.* God wants us to have many things which He will not give us unless we ask.

Jesus goes on to teach that we must not only ask, but we must ask insistently and persistently. He told the parable of the widow who kept hounding the heartless judge until finally to get rid of her he gave her justice. Then He made the application: "Will not God vindicate his elect, who cry to him day and night?" (Lk. 18:7).

This leads us to formulate our third rule: *Pray with persevering faith.* St. James writes: "Let him ask in faith, with no doubting, for he who doubts is like a wave of the sea, that is driven and tossed by the wind. For that person must not suppose that a double-minded man, unstable in all his ways, will receive anything from the Lord" (James 1:6 - 8).

To avoid confusion, let us take careful note of the difference between not being sure a thing is good for us (Rule One) and not being sure God is good enough to give us what is good for us (Rule Three). There are many times we are not sure a thing is good for us, and so God expects us to pray for it only provisionally. But there is never a time when God does not want us to have what is good for us, so He always wants us to pray without doubting.

There is too much poverty of body and soul in the world. Prayer of petition in accord with these biblical rules will help to lessen unnecessary poverty.

PART 4

28. Marriage Without Divorce

Why do marriages break up? What can be done to make your marriage happier and more secure?

Couples who fall in love want to stay in love, yet millions fail to keep their love alive. Why? What goes wrong? What makes enduring love an impossible dream for so many married couples? What secrets do the successfully married have? To find the answers I went to the true experts — I asked married couples themselves.

Let me begin with what I learned from a negative expert — a young man whose marriage quickly fell apart. His diagnosis was that he found out too late he wasn't ready for the responsibilities of marriage. He said it would have helped to live away from home for a while before marriage. He had been in the army, but he said that failed to help because the army was like a substitute mother.

A young single girl shared with me her reflections on marriage. "I have so many friends getting married this summer," she wrote. "It's hard to believe they want to get married so young. I just can't understand, maybe because I have always had it so nice at home that I'm not looking for an escape. I really believe that too many of my friends married because they couldn't wait to leave home. I want to take my time because I

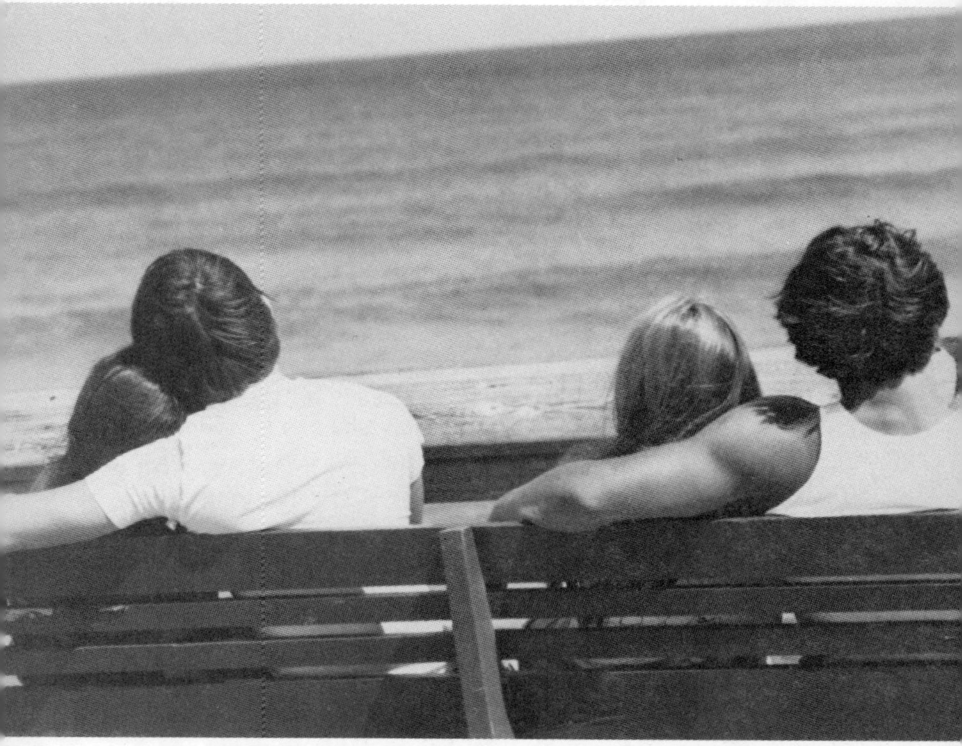

see how great my own parents get along and I admire them for their love and understanding of one another. I realize that it's an eternal relationship and something that will probably take the most consideration and thought of any decision I'll ever have to make."

From these two testimonials we can formulate the first two rules for Marriage Without Divorce: One: Before you say "I do," be sure you do face the responsibilities of married life. Two: Take the time to make the right choice the first time.

A husband who had celebrated the silver anniversary of his somewhat stormy but genuinely happy marriage told me that little spats helped. Arguments cleared the air, instead of allowing the pressure of secret resentments to build up. This gives us our third rule: Bring differences into the open or they may bring your marriage down in secret.

A happily married woman with two grandchildren gives us our fourth rule for a happy marriage. She said: "It takes two to work at it."

A woman married for more than thirty years in a somewhat difficult marriage told me that she experiences marriage as a friendship, partnership, and business. Each partner, she said, must respect the rights, the needs, and the individuality of the other. The woman, especially, must not be taken for granted. Our fifth rule is therefore: Problems in marriage must be worked out through compromise, just as in every other friendship, partnership, or business.

Seven years ago a friend of mine married a widow with four nearly grown children still at home. The marriage has been challenging, but the couple has been happy. I asked this man his secret for Marriage Without Divorce. He said simply: "To tell you the truth, I never thought about it. When we married it was FOR BETTER OR FOR WORSE." This Catholic man simply does not think of any alternative to staying married, but only how to make the best of his marriage. He gives us our sixth rule: Don't look for an alternative to your marriage. Divorce is no alternative; it is a failure of all alternatives.

To round out these testimonials, I went to a priest-theologian who specializes in marriage. When I asked him the secret of Marriage Without Divorce he said: "The lived love of the married couple must convince them that married love is by its very nature exclusive and undying, so that even to consider divorce is a kind of unfaithfulness. In true love they feel their love saying to them: I AM FOREVER. This goes back to God, whose love is undying faithfulness, and who communicated this to man and woman when He made them in His image and likeness." From this we have our seventh rule: Nature and nature's God teach that married love is a sacred trust which cannot be broken without tragic consequences.

One woman who teaches a course in marriage insists that, after God, a wife must give the highest priority to her husband. She reports that one husband complained he has not had a wife since their first child. Let me add that some husbands give their work such a high priority that their wives take second place. This leads us to our eighth rule: Not children, not career, but only God deserves higher priority than the marriage partner.

This same marriage teacher adds her rule of the Four A's: Accept, Admire, Appreciate and Adapt. Accept your husband for what he is and don't try to make him over. Admire some quality of your husband, admire it aloud in his presence — after all, he was wise enough to marry you! Appreciate and thank your husband at least now and then. Shakespeare's Lear said: "Ingratitude, thou marble-hearted fiend!" Adapt your lifestyle to your husband's, whom the Bible and the bulk of human experience recognize as the leader. Our ninth rule is: Keep the Four A's and the Four A's will keep your marriage.

Other experts point out that some marriages founder around unnecessarily exhausted wives. These are the housewives who squander their mornings on unnecessary tasks because they won't face up to the work that really needs doing. Late in the day they rush and strain over the necessary things. When their husbands arrive they have nothing for them but a tale of woe and overwork. The result is that very soon the husbands find reasons for coming home late. Our tenth rule is therefore: Plan your day to put first things first.

I would like to close with a few thoughts of my own: Marriage is a religious mystery. It is a consecration to God to share His love and bear His human children.

Marriage is also a mystery showing forth the Incarnation. Through the Incarnation God joined His Divinity to humanity in a kind of eternal marriage in the person of Jesus Christ. Jesus extends His Incarnation and mystical marriage to many others through baptism and Holy Communion, so that the whole Church becomes the bride of Christ.

The secret of Marriage Without Divorce is to imitate the love of the Heart of Jesus, the Divine Bridegroom. He loved when unloved. He loved and forgave even His killers. He died to save our lives and rose to give us life. The paschal mystery of His dying and rising gives us our eleventh and last Rule: Marriage without Divorce requires married couples to die to selfishness and live a life shared selflessly, as Jesus lived.

29. Is Patriotism a Museum Piece?

Is patriotism a worn-out holdover from other times? Do cooperative international efforts like the United Nations render patriotism obsolete?

On July 4, 1779 — only three years after the signing of the Declaration of Independence — Catholics gathered for a patriotic religious service in St. Mary's Church in downtown Philadelphia, very near Independence Hall. They were celebrating Independence Day. Do we still deem patriotism a virtue worthy of being honored and urged by the Church? Or is patriotism a museum piece, practiced only by the politically simplistic and the political dinosaurs who do not see that nationalism is dying and yielding to a world order?

To answer those questions, let us ask another: What is patriotism? The word *patriot* is a direct takeover from the Latin *patriota* and the Greek *patriotes*. The basic meaning of both words was simply *fellow-countryman*. Those words carried that meaning thousands of years ago, and to this day a patriot is basically simply a genuine fellow citizen. Genuine, because the patriot is one who loves his country and can be relied on to be loyal to it and defend it in need.

The ancients had a deep reverence for patriotism because they saw how it fitted into a human being's enduring relationship to his origins. A man's origins are his God, his parents, and his country. They give him his being, his birth, and his culture. God, family, and country have such a claim on a man's loyalty that no man can refuse to pay it without bankrupting himself. A man is what he has inherited from God, father, and fatherland. To betray them is to become a traitor to himself. It is to cut his own roots and languish. Sir Walter Scott captures this truth in his words:

> Breathes there the man with soul so dead
> Who never to himself hath said,
> This is my own, my native land!

To his three roots of God, father, and fatherland, a man owes a joint fidelity which the ancients called *pietas*, piety. To be pious meant to be truly filial; it meant to be a loyal son or daughter of one's God, home, and homeland. Piety makes a person religious, family-loving, and patriotic.

If patriotism is understood in this way, it can never become obsolete. Our fatherland is one of the gifts from the Father of all that should lead us back to Him. It is also a motherland, a sisterland, and a brotherland. It joins us to a vast community of people with whom we share a common destiny and experience common concerns.

To say that patriotism is for all ages is not to say that it does not have to grow and be updated in each age. Our age is an age which demands its updating. The world is growing closer together, and international bonds are necessarily multiplying. Patriotism must deal intelligently with the reality of these new unities. For the genuine patriot this is not overly difficult, for citizenship has given him practice in nearly universal brotherhood, and so it is a school in which he learns to love all mankind. The man who genuinely loves his countrymen also loves all others, for love cannot be walled in. Furthermore, every man is a member of both his country and his world, and responsible for the good of both as he is dependent on the good of both. There is no enlightened nationalism without some degree of internationalism. The genuine patriot, then, is not blind, narrow, or prejudiced. He is a lover of mankind who gives his country the special love and loyalty he owes it.

The man who thinks he loves the world but does not love his own country is not genuine. If a man does not even love those who have given him everything he has, how can he love those who have given him nothing? That is why I say that the man who loves the world but not his own country is far more prejudiced than the man who loves his own country but not the world.

Nationalism and internationalism are complementary, not contradictory. They do go together, and they must go together. Devoted love of country is not incompatible with a devoted love of the United Nations, any more than love of family and Church are incompatible with love of country. Because of our experience in this twofold loyalty to Church and country, we Christians should be able to lead the way to a United Nations. The bishops of the last Ecumenical Council wrote: "The Christian faithful (are) gathered together in the Church out of all nations. . . . As good citizens they should practice true and effective patriotism. At the same time, let them altogether avoid bitter nationalism, fostering instead a universal love for men" (Decree on the Missions, No. 15).

Jesus Himself is the model of both patriotism and internationalism. He loved all men, but he had a special feeling for His own country. When He looked at Jerusalem and prophetically foresaw its destruction, He cried.

Jesus also taught the proper relationship of patriotism to religion. Love of country must serve love of God, not usurp it. Jesus told us to give the government what we owe it, and to give God what we owe Him. In His own words: "Give to Caesar what is Caesar's, but give to God what is God's" (Mk. 12:17).

Patriotism is a good worth praying for, so I have composed the following prayer: "Father of all fathers, we ask You to touch our hearts with the Spirit of love for our families and friends, our home and homeland. Stir our appreciation, stir our faithfulness, stir in us the love that responds to our country's needs.

"You have given us a country that ranges from ocean to ocean, and a people gathered from all peoples, and a nation whose freedom is a byword round the world. You have given us a young nation with a long roster of heroes echoing across the centuries from George Washington and Patrick Henry to Abraham Lincoln and John F. Kennedy. You have given us a land of which to be proud, though we as a nation have done much of which to be ashamed.

"Purify our nation. Make it worthy of its greatest patriots, living and dead. Purify our hearts. Make them fit for service to so fine a land and to a people hungry for that eternal freedom which only You can give. Help us make our land a brotherland and sisterland to all peoples, sharing its abundance with those who have too little. Guide us to establishment of laws and legislation that will root out such evils as abortion, and make our country an instrument of Your holy will and Your kingdom on earth and Your concern for all men. Enhance our religious freedom. Make us patriots to our homeland on earth, and make us patriots to that homeland of all homelands in heaven where You have enrolled us as fellow citizens forever. Amen."

30. Thank God for the Pope!

What is the source of our religious truth? Where would we Catholics be without obedience to our Bishop and Pope?

Of the many bad attitudes common in the world today, one of the worst is the attitude that authority is a nasty thing. The fact is that in matters of truth, authority is our firmest hope. Therefore, the widespread refusal to accept the teaching of our bishops and popes is an attack on faith.

Where would we be without the guidance of the Catholic hierarchy? The Chair of Peter has guarded Christian truth for almost two thousand years. When Christians in or out of the Catholic Church separate themselves from the Chair of Peter they begin taking stands against one another on almost every Christian truth and almost every moral concern — thus confusing the teaching of Christ and splintering the effect we have on the conduct of men. Yet St. Paul said there is only "one faith," and we know he is right. Without the popes and bishops we Catholics, like other divided Christians, would not know what to believe.

Someone might object: "Oh, but Jesus said: 'They will all be taught by God' (Jn. 6:45). So I'm taught by God — I have no need of a pope and bishops."

My answer to that objection is this: I too believe that I am taught by God and His Holy Spirit, for Jesus said it was so. But I am taught by God to go to the Church and to the Pope and bishops to learn the truth. Scripture says the truth comes "by hearing" (Rom. 10:17 NAT). Look through the whole New Testament — and look in vain — for one case of anyone converted to Christianity by the inner word of God's Spirit alone. Even when St. Paul had his vision on the road to Damascus, Jesus told him to go to Ananias — that is, to the Church — to learn what to do.

The same Jesus who said we would be taught by God also said we would be taught by the men He put in charge of His Church, and He said we must listen and obey. To His apostle Simon he gave a new name: *Cephas* in Aramaic, *Petros* in Greek, and *Peter* in English. The name means *rock*. And Jesus said to Peter: "You are Peter, and on this rock I will build my Church. . . . I will give you the keys of the kingdom of heaven, and whatever you bind on earth shall be bound in heaven, and whatever you loose on earth shall be loosed in heaven" (Mt. 16:18 - 19). And Jesus said to the Eleven after His resurrection: "Go into all the whole world and preach the Gospel to the whole creation. He who believes and is baptized will be saved; but he who does not believe will be condemned" (Mk. 16:15 - 16). This is the teaching of Jesus. Thus I believe in the Pope and bishops, not just because they tell me I must but because the Word of God in the Scriptures and the Spirit of God in my heart tell me I must.

A Catholic priest in a small town in North Carolina had a non-Catholic friend named Benny. Benny used to go to the park and preach Christ. And he would say: "You know, when our Founding Fathers wrote the Constitution, they knew they couldn't let everybody interpret it for himself, or there would be bedlam. So they appointed the Supreme Court to interpret it. Now," Benny went on, "Jesus Christ was smarter than our Founding Fathers. He does not allow anyone to interpret the Scriptures as he pleases. He appointed the Pope to interpret for everyone." That was Benny's message. The years passed and finally Benny lay dying. Father Andy said to him "Don't you want to become a Catholic?" "Yes," said Benny. "Why did you wait so long?" asked Father Andy. "Because I wasn't worthy," said Benny.

Are we worthy of the Church and the hierarchy God has given us? Do we attack it or reverently obey it, as simply as children? Surely, Jesus had this need for humble obedience in mind when He said: "I bless you Father, Lord of heaven and earth, for hiding these things from the learned and the clever of this world and revealing them to the merest children" (Mt. 11:25 J). There are many learned and clever men who teach all sorts of dissension and division and distortion of Christian truth, and who give it the fancy name "dogmatic pluralism." But this distorted teaching cannot save, for only God's truth can save. Such teaching is divisive. Only the teaching of Jesus can make us one. Jesus yearns to make us all one. He yearns to have us obedient to the truth and to the Father and to legitimate human authority, just as He was. He loved authority, for true authority leads to God the Author of life. Jesus said: "My food is to do the will of the one who sent me . . ." (Jn. 14:23). He wants us to keep His word as it is interpreted by those He set over us in the Church.

This is no new teaching. One of the earliest bishops after the Apostles was St. Ignatius of Antioch. He wrote to the Trallians as follows: "Abstain from plants of alien growth, that is, heresy. . . . He that does anything apart from bishop, priesthood and deacon has no pure conscience."

And St. Augustine wrote 1500 years ago: "When the Devil saw the human race abandoning the temples of demons . . . in the name of the freedom-giving Mediator (that is, Jesus) he inspired heretics to oppose Christian teaching under cover of the Christian name as though their presence in the City of God could go unchallenged, like the presence, in the City of confusion, of philosophers with . . . contradictory opinions!" No, the Devil's deceits and the deceits of confused Christians cannot and do not go unchallenged. Salvation is from God alone, and He guards the purity of His word through the Pope and bishops, who are guided by His Holy Spirit so that they may neither add nor subtract from the Revelation. And so I say, "Thank God for the Pope!"

But it isn't only Catholics who thank God for the Pope. Many other Christians listen to him, and some feel closer to him than to their own denomination. And he certainly feels close to them. Pope Paul once said: "Ah, Churches of Christ, so distant from us and yet so near! How deep are our feelings of good will toward you. How incessant is our concern for you! How our tears well up as we long to honor and embrace you in Christ's fraternal love!"

Today a number of Churches, but especially Episcopalians and Lutherans, are working with Catholics to find a unity under the Pope that is acceptable to them. For they too are aware that Christ prayed the night before He died "that they may all be one" (Jn. 17:21). And so, as the struggle for Christian unity continues, I continue to pray for the day that all Christians will thank God for the Pope.

31. Questions Men Ask God

Why does God permit thieves, murderers and suppressors of religion to roam the world unhampered? Is there any answer to this question?

We live in times which both try our faith and mock our faithfulness. Not only does sin openly abound in our society, but the notion of calling it sin is scorned. The clever crook is praised in our stories, while adultery is taken for granted and marriage considered old-fashioned.

Surrounded by such a maelstrom of evil, we naturally wonder about Divine providence. We ask Why? Why? Why does God permit it all? Why does He not put an end to it? We sometimes ask these questions rhetorically, as though we were hopelessly in the dark, poor little sheep without an answer to our pitiful bleating. This is completely false. The Bible gives answers to our questions.

Let us look at the answers of the Old Testament first. The Book of Wisdom of Solomon addresses God and says: "Thou dost correct little by little those who trespass, and dost remind and warn them . . . that they may be freed from wickedness and put their trust in thee" (12:2). So the first answer the Bible

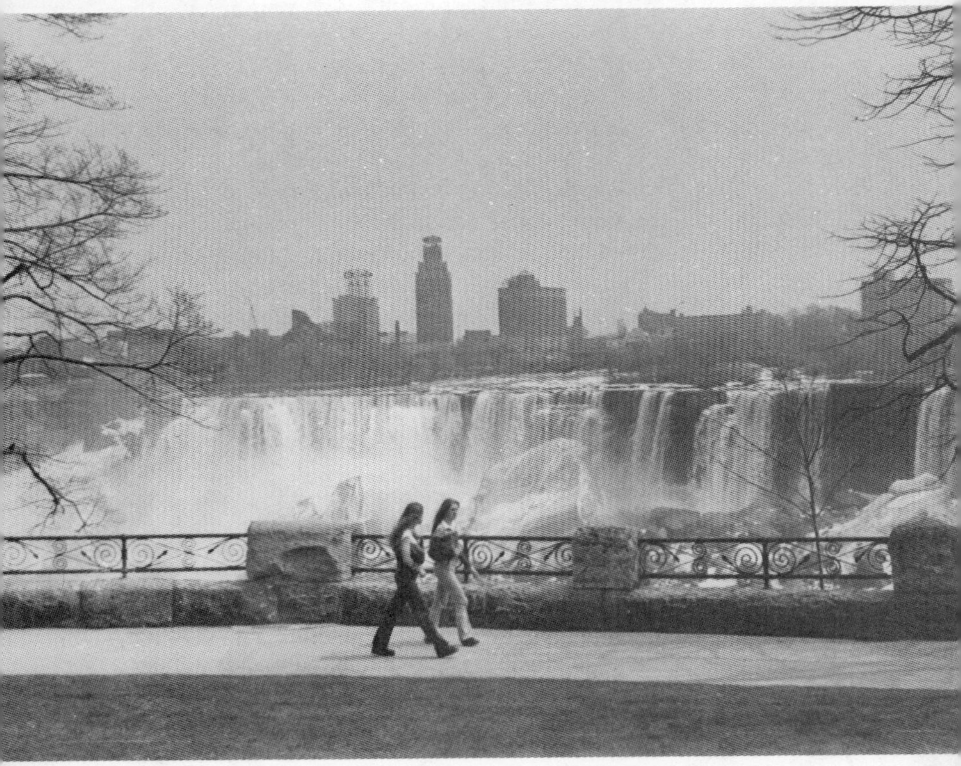

gives us is this: God is patient with the evil in the world for the sake of the enemies of God, to give them time to repent and become His friends. The Book of Wisdom goes on to make three more points: The first is that by extending his kindness to all, even to those who do not deserve it, God teaches His people to be kind. The second is that by showing such mercy, even to rebellious sinners, God gives His children all the more assurance that their sins of weakness will be forgiven. Third, God reminds us that He owes us no explanation of the way He conducts world affairs. The Wisdom of Solomon makes this point when it says to God: "Who will say 'What hast thou done?' Or who will resist thy judgment? Who will accuse thee . . .? For neither is there any god beside thee . . . to whom thou shouldst prove that thou hast not judged unjustly" (12:12 - 13). In other words, who is there capable of judging the judgments of God? God's judgments are final. He owes an explanation to no one.

The New Testament gives us further answers to the problem of evil. At the Last Supper Jesus said: "No longer do I call you servants, for the servant does not know what his master is doing; but I have called you friends, for all that I have heard from my Father I have made known to you" (Jn. 15:15). And Jesus has made known to us the reasons why God permits evil. In the parable of the weeds He has given us an explanation of why God allows evildoers to go on.

That parable contains a whole theology of history:

> The kingdom of heaven may be compared to a man who sowed good seed in his field; but while men were sleeping, his enemy came and sowed weeds among the wheat, and went away. So when the plants came up and bore grain, then the weeds appeared also. And the servants of the householder came and said to him, "Sir, did you not sow good seed in your field? How then has it weeds?" He said to them, "An enemy has done this." The servants said to him, "Then do you want us to go and gather them up?" But he said, "No, lest in gathering the weeds you root up the wheat along with them. Let both grow together until

the harvest; and at harvest time I will tell the reapers, Gather the weeds first and bind them in bundles to be burned, but gather the wheat into my barn" (Mt. 13:24 - 30).

What if, in this parable of the weeds, when the servants said, "Do you want us to pull up the weeds?" the owner said, "Yes"? Let me describe such a world without weeds by a parable of my own: I call it "The Parable of the World of Justice." The parable runs as follows:

A father prayed to God to rid the world of evildoers. Then he sat down to dinner with his family. He asked where his oldest son was, and his youngest boy said: "He's not coming home any more. He was stealing a car and just as he turned on the ignition, Zap, a lightning bolt came down and burned him to a cinder — just the way it used to happen to the aliens in that TV story, *The Invaders!*" Then there was a knock on the door and a policeman said: "Your married daughter was committing adultery and Zap, a lightning bolt passed right through the roof and burned up both her and her lover."

Terribly shaken, the father turned on the radio for some quiet music, and he heard the following announcement: "The President is calling a special meeting to choose new appointees for the Supreme Court. The former members, just an hour ago, voted in favor of legalized abortion, and a fire storm from the sky struck the whole building and turned them to white-hot torches that burned up and disappeared."

That is my parable. Now my question: Would you like to live in a world where these things went on constantly? It would be a gestapo state. Even the good people would be terrified. We wouldn't need a police force, but we would need many more psychiatrists — if we didn't get zapped ourselves! That is why Jesus says in His parable that the evil are spared for the sake of the good: for their peace, for their great trust in God's patient kindness. After considering this parable, I'm glad to live in the world we know, despite its evil!

But there is another point the Parable of Jesus makes, for

it is the word of God, and the word of God is a two-edged sword that brings great hope to us if we are faithful but strikes fear in us if we begin to be evil ourselves. This first point, implicit in Jesus' parable, is as follows: If God lets His faithful suffer so much, what punishment does He have stored up for sinners who to the end deliberately choose to rebel against Him? In explaining His own parable, Jesus says that the weeds are evil men planted by the devil, and He says that at the end of the world the angels will "throw them into the furnace of fire; there men will weep and gnash their teeth" (Mt. 13:42). And the First Letter of Peter says: "Beloved, do not be surprised at the fiery ordeal which comes upon you to prove you. . . . For the time has come for the judgment to begin with the household of God; and if it begins with us, what will be the end of those who do not obey the Gospel of God?" (1 Peter 4:12, 17).

We see, then, that God does answer our question, why? Why evil? Why suffering? He tells us that even the suffering He sends us is a part of His faithfulness to us, for it preserves us sinners from worse evils. The psalmist, who understood this, teaches us to say: "I know O Lord that thy judgments are right, and that in faithfulness thou hast afflicted me" (Ps. 119:75).

32. How Can I Stop Being Angry?

Does the spiritual life teach us how to control our anger? Does devotion to the Heart of Jesus teach us patience?

We are all familiar with the harm done by anger. It turns husbands and wives bitter toward one another. It produces hatred between parents and children. It makes our houses places we hate to come home to. It gives us no peace. It kills the things we love. The Bible says: "Better is a dinner of herbs where love is than a fatted ox and hatred with it" (Prov. 15:17).

We can work the miracle of taming our anger, but we have to pay the price in effort. The only price some people want to pay is a cheap act of the will. They say impatiently: "I'll never get angry again!" — and they are already angry about getting angry in the past. Getting angry about being angry gets them nowhere.

We cannot control our emotions simply by an act of the will, but we can gradually subdue them by the use of our minds. We can draw up a reasoned program for the control of anger. And so I have drawn up a "Seven Day Program For Patience." For each day, I suggest one practice together with a Bible passage to be recited during that day. I do not promise anyone patience in a week, but I look for an encouraging improvement in a week. In the following weeks, one simply repeats the program. In a few months, it will become a habit, a part of one's way of life.

The first reason some people get angry and spout off is that they are constantly on edge. Their emotional life is like a boiling pot. One additional degree of upset and they blow their lids! The first practice, therefore, is to get rid of rushing around — to get rid of anxiety in our lives. Cultivate peace. Slow down. Even God rested on the last day of the week. We Christians have been led to rest on the first day of the week, Sunday.

The practice for Sunday is to rest and cultivate calmness. The Bible passage to memorize, and recite during the day, are the words of Jesus: "I tell you, do not be anxious about your life, what you shall eat, nor about your body, what you shall put on" (Lk. 12:22). Remember, this is the Lord's command. Give up anxiety and rushing, for they are destructive. Soon peace will grow. This is the first step to patience.

At noon and again at night, I should examine myself: Did I say the Bible passage frequently, and try to put it into practice? If so, I thank God; if not, I tell God I am sorry and will do better tomorrow. I use this twice-daily examen for each day's practice.

The practice for Monday is to ask God's help to overcome

my anger. We need God's help for everything, and we need assurance from Him that we can succeed. To get his help and assurance, I repeat through the day the words of Jesus: "Ask, and it will be given to you; seek, and you will find" (Mt. 7:7). I ask Him for patience, and tell Him I am not only asking but doing my part by seeking patience through my Seven-Day Program.

On Tuesday, we consider the cause of impatience and the cure for it. Here I report a personal experience which helped me to grow much in patience.

I was struggling with my impatience when one day I learned the root meaning of the word impatience. The word comes from the Latin word *impatiens* which means *unwilling to suffer*. That is really what impatience is: an unwillingness to suffer. I had been telling Jesus that in devotion to His Sacred Heart I wanted to make reparation to Him by sharing His passion, His *patiens*, His willingness to suffer. And, in fact, each time someone or something brought suffering into my life, I was impatient, I was angry and tried to thrust it out of my life. This discovery of my refusal to suffer — to suffer with Jesus — shamed me, and I resolved to recognize in temptations to impatience an opportunity to share in the passion of Christ. Ever since, I have been far less impatient. Therefore, the Tuesday practice is to recall the passion of Jesus, meditate on it, and repeat through the day the loving words of St. Paul: "I rejoice in my sufferings . . . in my flesh I complete what is lacking in Christ's afflictions for the sake of his body, that is, the church . . ." (Col. 1:24).

Wednesday is the day to think about the fact that our anger is often unjust. We blame someone, and then discover it is we who were at fault. And even when the other person was at fault, our anger may do more harm to him than his fault did to us. The practice for Wednesday is to grow in the realization that anger usually does more harm than good. And the biblical thought for Wednesday is that "the anger of man does not work the righteousness of God" (James 1:20).

Thursday is the day to abandon ourselves to Divine providence. Instead of raging against those who have some power over us and use it unjustly, we try to realize that no one can do anything to us unless God permits it, and if He permits it, He will make it come out to our advantage in the end. To help us see that no one can do anything unless God permits it, we repeat on Thursday the words of Jesus to His persecutor, Pontius Pilate: "You would have no power over me unless it had been given you from above" (Jn. 19:11).

On Friday, we remember how much we constantly need forgiveness from God and from our family and friends for our own faults. We reflect on this, and see that we ought to be afraid not to be patient and forgiving of the faults of others, lest God refuse to forgive us. And the biblical words we repeat on Friday are the words from the Our Father: "Forgive us our trespasses as we forgive those who trespass against us." And we may find it helpful to add the words which Jesus kept repeating as His Body was nailed to the Cross: "Father, forgive them; for they know not what they do" (Lk. 23:34).

On Saturday, we think about the Mother of God and of us all. How tender and forgiving she is! How readily she endured whatever God sent her way! We make our own her attitude and her biblical words: "Behold, I am the handmaid of the Lord. Let it be done to me according to your word." By imitating Mary we can make people trust in God's forgiveness as she did. For people say: "If she is so forgiving how forgiving God must be!" And so we will be truly God's image, giving Him glory by our patience and forgiveness.

This is my seven-day plan for cultivating patience in the Lord. By God's grace, it can help us put on the mind and heart of Christ. It can help us to bring a little more peace into our lives, into our families — and into the world.

33. Don't Waste Your Sufferings!

Can we profit from our sufferings instead of getting despondent about them? Does God really make good use of our sickness and suffering?

Last time I was down with the flu it occurred to me that sickness is to the soul what waste products are to the land. Sickness is the environmental pollutant of the soul. And at once I saw how God has taken the initiative in offering to dispose of this environmental pollution. The following parable illustrates God's way of acting.

One day a certain manufacturer stands looking forlornly at the mountain of waste products outside his factory. A stranger comes up and asks: "Why is that mountain of refuse sitting there?" The owner replies: "Because I can't afford to have that worthless heap removed. And in the meantime it's practically removing me from my own property!" The stranger says: "Worthless? You obviously are not keeping up with developments. There is a new conglomerate called TOMORROW'S ENTERPRISES. One of its subsidiaries is named BRICK ENERGY COMPANY. They pay you to carry your refuse away. They burn it to produce electrical energy, and then they use the cinders to produce bricks. Here is their card."

We are like that manufacturer. We have our waste products of pain and sickness and death. They are the most unwelcome of all environmental pollutants — and yet Christ the Son of God has made them invaluable. He uses them to burn away sin, and He converts them into building blocks for the kingdom of God. This conversion is possible to Him alone — and so only He finds use for these most useless of all waste products.

In this age of ecology, the lesson is clear. We should not let our sufferings go to waste. We should not let them accumulate in ugly mountains of groans and complaints which turn our

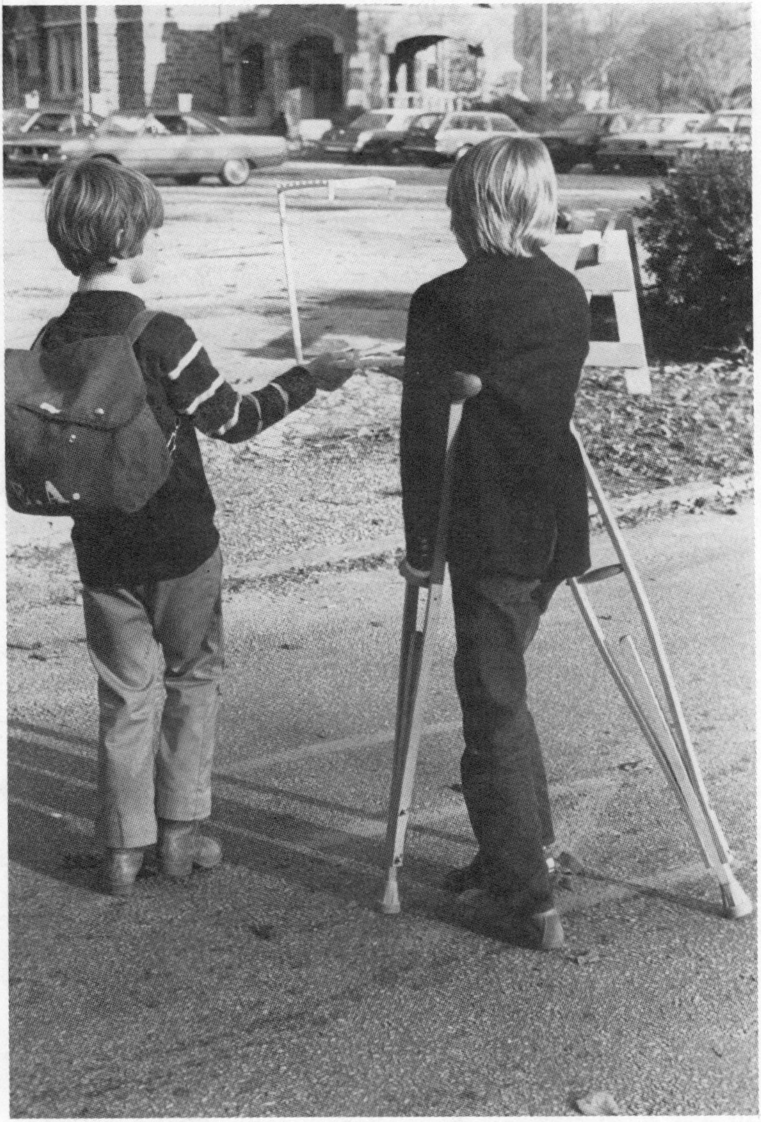

lives into unsightly bogs that no one comes near unless he must.

We can be good spiritual business persons. We begin by minimizing spiritual waste products. We live industrious and well-planned lives so that we do not foolishly cause ourselves suffering that is beyond our power to endure. Having done this, we turn to the job of making preparation beforehand to convert our inevitable sufferings into spiritually priceless products. How? By often considering the sufferings of Christ Jesus. Then we will see ever more clearly how Jesus suffered and died — not uselessly, but to save us from useless suffering and endless death. And then and there we offer Him our own future sufferings as products He needs to complete His work of redeeming the world.

If we follow this procedure, our lives will be a triumph of spiritual ecology. We will never accumulate depressing spiritual waste products. When suffering and death come — and come they will — they will continuously be converted into spiritual energy and into building blocks for the kingdom of God. For we will, in the words of St. Paul, "have this mind" among ourselves which is "in Christ Jesus, who, though he was in the form of God . . . emptied himself . . . and became obedient unto death . . ." (Phil. 2:5 - 8). What is this triumph of spiritual ecology? It is — in Jesus Christ — the conversion of suffering and death into the resurrection from the dead which we will share with Him.

34. Why Do I Need the Church?

If someone asked you why you need the Church, what would you answer?

Some years ago I stepped into a hospital room to see a certain woman who had dropped out of the Church. When I broached the subject she said: "What do I need the Church for?"

Her question has stuck with me, and if she is listening, I would like to give her a fuller answer than I was prepared to give that day. I would like to give my answer to all who are asking that same question.

We need the Church because it is the Divinely appointed herald who cries out to us the Good News of Jesus the Lord. The Church reveals to us that God Himself has come to save us — that the Word was made Man and dwelt among us — and that He took a share in our humanity to offer us a share in His Divinity.

The Church is the maternal womb in which I was given that share in Christ's Divinity — was born a son of God in baptism. The Church baptized me as Jesus instructed her to do when He said: "Go into the whole world and proclaim the good news to all creation. The man who believes in it and accepts baptism will be saved" (Mk. 16:15 - 16 NAT).

The Church is the Mother who cures my worldly blindness by faithfully teaching me the fullness of the teaching of Jesus. She teaches me right from wrong; she teaches me what serves God and what sins against God. She teaches me to renounce the world's despair and unbelief and put my trust in the living God. She teaches me with the authority of Christ, who said to Peter the first Pope: "Whatever you declare bound on earth shall be bound in heaven; whatever you declare loosed on earth shall be loosed in heaven" (Mt. 16:19 NAT).

The Church is the brotherhood and sisterhood in whose company I walk on pilgrimage to our true homeland. It is the people who believe in God as I believe, and hope in Christ as I hope, and are inspired by His Holy Spirit to love God and His creation as I am inspired to love them. We are the people who live biblical morality in all matters, and who with sorrow confess our sins to the priest when we fail. We believe in the priestly power to forgive sins in God's name because the risen Jesus breathed on His Apostles and said: "Receive the Holy

Spirit. If you forgive men's sins they are forgiven them" (Jn. 20:23 NAT).

The Church is the handmaid of God who ministers to a world sick with selfishness and injustice. And the Church is the teacher who teaches me to minister as she does.

The Church is the one who tells me of Christ not merely by preaching but by pointing to her saints. And she not only teaches me of Christ, she joins me to Christ by her sacraments, above all by the Eucharist. Of that bread of angels and wine of God Jesus Himself said: "He who feeds on my flesh and drinks my blood has life eternal, and I will raise him up on the last day" (Jn. 6:54 NAT).

When the woman in the hospital asked me what need she had for the Church, I did not think of all these things. What did flash through my mind is the thought that Easter was only a few days away, and that I had just been feeding sick people with the risen body of Christ in Holy Communion. And so I said to her: "We have the body of Christ. What do you have?"

35. Frequent Confession Yesterday, Today, and Tomorrow

Is frequent use of the Sacrament of Penance still recommended by the Church? Or should we refrain from bothering the priest unless we have serious sins to confess?

Some time ago a woman whose holiness I had learned to respect told me about a recent confession experience. The confessor had more or less told her not to waste his time with her trivial faults. In effect he had advised her against frequent confession. His advice had made her uneasy, and she was wisely seeking another opinion.

I was able to inform her that already back in the 1940s

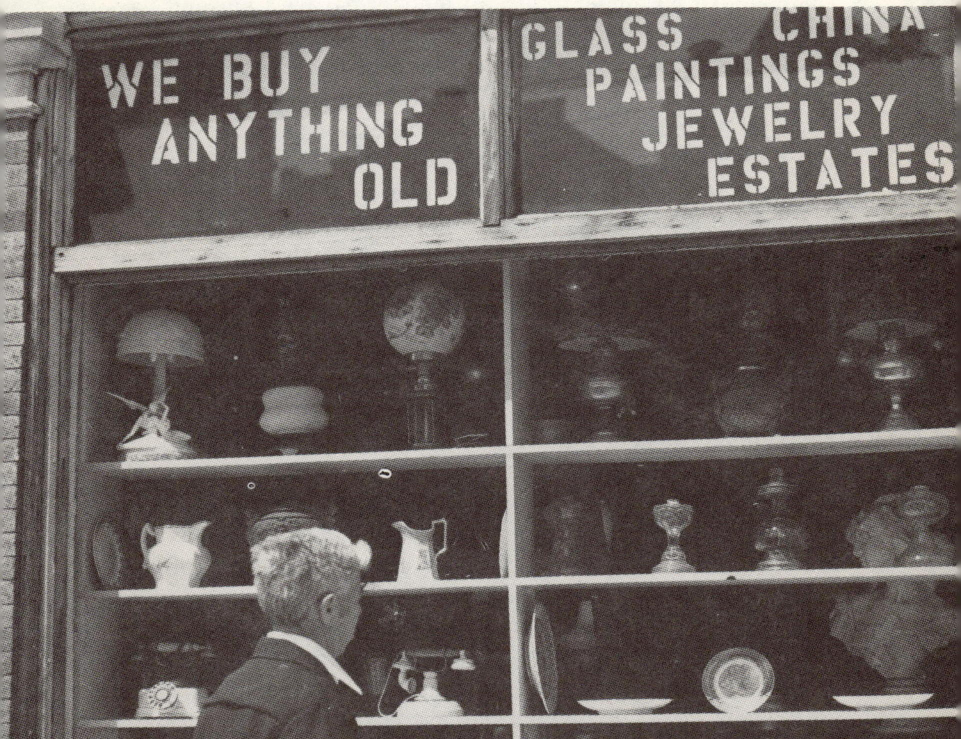
WE BUY
ANYTHING
OLD
GLASS CHINA
PAINTINGS
JEWELRY
ESTATES

Pope Pius XII had condemned such advice. In his encyclical *Mystici Corporis* he wrote: "Let those among the young clergy who make light of or weaken esteem for frequent confession realize that what they are doing is foreign to the Spirit of Christ and disastrous for the Mystical Body of our Savior."

In a way, the roots of the practice of frequent confession go back to the Apostles of Jesus. They confessed their sins to Him daily by living out all their faults right in front of His eyes. And by frequent confession saintly Catholics have long imitated what they did.

Someone may wish to object that all this is out-of-date, that we are no longer morbidly concerned with sin and have new ideas. I will admit that ours is an age in which sin is ignored, denied, and unconfessed. Yet it remains as true as ever that only the man who admits his sins can claim Jesus for Savior. As to the claim that frequent confession is out-of-date, let me quote Pope Paul's answer, given in 1975 in his Apostolic Exhortation "On Christian Joy": "What burden is more crushing than that of sin? . . . Following the line of the best spiritual tradition, we remind the faithful and their pastors that the confessing of grave sins is necessary and that frequent confession remains a privileged source of holiness, peace and joy."

Let me add an observation of my own as a confessor. I have noticed that people who confess often are generally extremely sensitive to their slightest offense against God, just as any two people very much in love feel deeply the slightest falling out and want to make up as soon as possible. People who confess infrequently incline to be at least a little hard of heart. They tend to take venial sins for granted and have little sorrow for them and little intention of improving. And people who rarely come to confession tend to have half-dead consciences. Even when they are doing badly they are inclined to think they are doing quite well. They are like a captain with a ship so encrusted with barnacles for so long that he has long since forgotten how sleek and fast his ship used to be.

Frequent confession has many advantages — too many for

me to list them all. Let me just quote Pope Pius XII, who wrote that by frequent confession "genuine self-knowledge is increased, Christian humility grows, bad habits are corrected . . . the will is strengthened . . . and grace is increased in virtue of the sacrament itself" *(Mystici Corporis)*.

Even from the realm of psychiatry we have a confirmation of the health value of confession. The renowned psychiatrist Carl Jung wrote: "Confessions to one's secret self are almost useless; to another, much more promising."

From what I have said and the sources I have used it is evident that not only my own experience but the highest authority in the Church continues to teach the value of frequent confession. So we are faced with pressing matter for examination of conscience! As the world continually tries to blackjack our consciences, are we guarding sensitivity to God's will by frequent confession?

PART 5

36. Instant Independence

Who is the real slave and who the real free man? What must you possess to be genuinely independent?

Recently on a drive through the Pennsylvania countryside, I spotted a billboard proclaiming the words: INSTANT INDEPENDENCE! I read on. The message was: "Play the Pennsylvania lottery!" That advertisement led me to reflect on the philosophy behind the lottery. It comes to this, that many people take a chance of becoming a little poorer so that one lucky winner might become instantly rich.

Then this question occurred to me: What if there were one man so wealthy that if he became poor it would make everyone rich? And what if that man did just that — impoverished himself to make us all rich?

Truth is stranger than fiction. There is such a man. St. Paul describes Him to the Corinthians: "You know the grace of our Lord Jesus Christ, that though He was rich, yet for your sake He became poor, so that by His poverty you might become rich" (2 Cor. 8:9). The lottery provides a one-in-a-million chance of financial independence, but Jesus Christ provides an absolutely certain opportunity for every kind of independence. The truth of that statement will become more evident if we inquire into the nature of independence.

What is true slavery and what is true independence? Some people might say that poverty is the worst slavery, yet Jesus Christ freely chose to be poor and that did not make Him a slave to anything. True slavery is the slavery to sin. Sin dethrones reason in its rule over our lives and puts us into slavery to our passions. Furthermore, sin hands us over to eternal death, and that is the ultimate slavery. Is this not our real poverty? We are poor in innocence. We are poor in life. Yet the Book of Wisdom assures us that "God did not make death" (1:13). God made man in His own image — that is, immortal. He made man rich in life. It was sin and not God that made death. By sin man stripped off his godliness and therefore his immortality. Death came through the devil who drew men to sin.

The message of the Bible is that Jesus restores our godliness and therefore our immortality. To the Sadducees who did not believe in the resurrection Jesus said: "You are wrong, because you know neither the scriptures nor the power of God" (Mt. 22:29). Jesus Himself is the Anointed One promised by the Scriptures. He *is* the power of God. To His friends Jesus said: "I am the resurrection and the life" (Jn. 11:25).

This is what Jesus is all about: He is our independence from sin and death. This is what Christianity is all about: independence from death. Toward the end of his life Paul was imprisoned, and he gave witness and said: "I am on trial before you today because of the resurrection of the dead" (Acts 24:21 NAT). We are all undergoing that trial. If our faith in the independence promised through the resurrection is weak, we will be enslaved to money and other things. But if we have strong belief and hope in Jesus our Resurrection, we will take His advice and invest our money in eternal life by acts of love and generous living.

When we believed in Jesus we were given instant independence from sin and death. If we hold fast to Him we will be given the ultimate independence: immortality. That is real freedom. That is genuine independence. Nothing else is.

37. Prayer Is Not for Simpletons

Since God knows what we need before we ask Him, is there any need to ask favors of Him? Does prayer of petition make any sense?

Prayer of petition is at the heart of true religion. That is why it is tragic when intelligent people posing as religious experts discourage people who pray for favors. These false experts object to prayer of petition by saying: God knows our needs before we ask Him. So why ask?

By this objection these objectors display their own terribly underdeveloped religious sense. It is necessary to expose their religious immaturity to ward off the harm they do to simple and innocent believers.

A story will expose the worthlessness of their objection. A mother had two daughters. The first said: "Mother, your hair is lovely. Would you set mine the same way?" Her mother answered: "Of course, dear. Right now." The second daughter moped around and one day burst out: "You set my sister's hair, but not mine!" The mother replied: "But you didn't ask!" "Yes," the daughter retorted, "but you knew I wanted it!" "My dear," her mother replied, "to know is one thing. To be asked is another. You, too, knew I like being asked when you want a favor. You knew, but did not ask. And now, come on, I'll set your hair too."

Our false experts do not understand that God acts toward us much like that mother. They erroneously picture Him like some heavenly computer programmed to know all our needs and to automatically say "yes" to some and "no" to others. They have not known God as Father. They have not approached Him as He likes to be approached, and discussed their needs with Him, and come to a mutual understanding. They have not haggled with Him like Abraham and wrestled

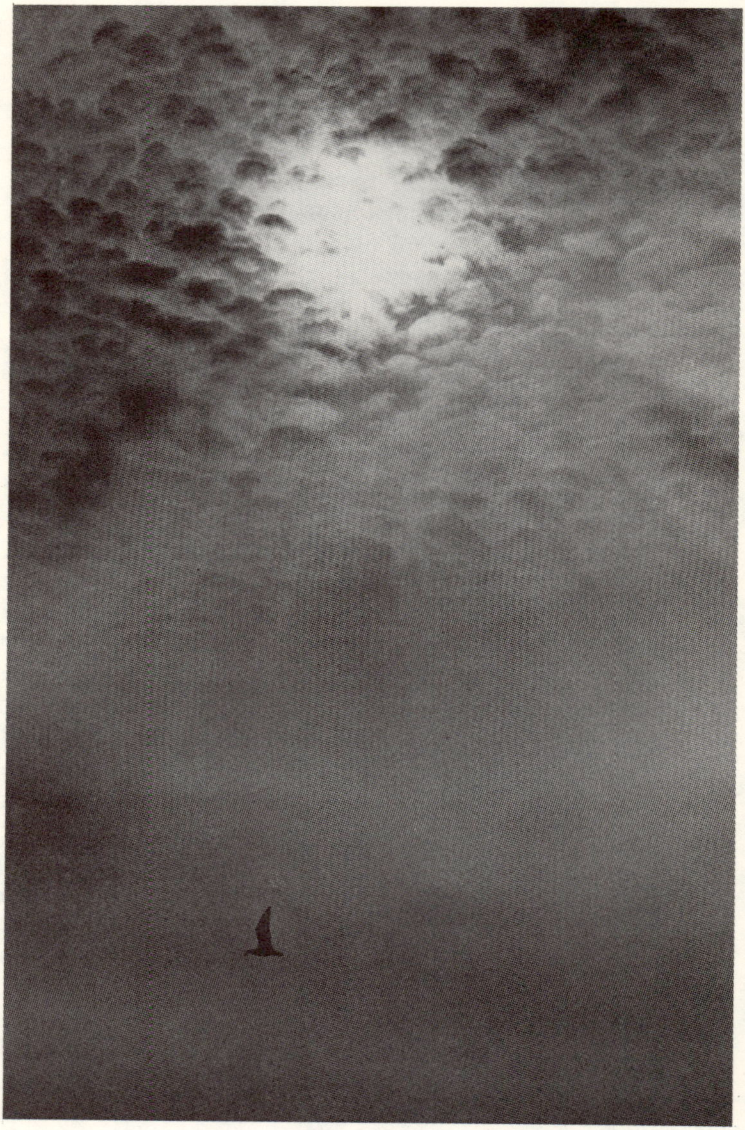

with Him like Jacob, and gone to Him in confidence like Jesus. Jesus made the role of a father the basis of His teaching on prayer. He said: "In praying do not heap up empty phrases as the Gentiles do . . . for your Father knows what you need before you ask him. Pray then like this. . . ." And then Jesus gave us that great prayer of praise and petition, the Our Father.

Our relationship with God, then, is like our human relationships. It is very personal, very living, very complex, and very mysterious. Like the mother in my story, God likes to be asked, wants to be asked, demands to be asked. After all, our human feelings, which make us hate being taken for granted, are in some way a copy of God's Divine nature, for we are made in His image and likeness.

There is another reason God wants us to ask His help. Asking helps to remind not Him but us of our dependence on Him. To those who would call this a childish dependence let me object in turn that there is a difference between being childish and being childlike. To be childish is to act like children when we ought not; to be childlike is to act like children when in truth we are no more than children. And so it is that the wisest men commonly show themselves the most childlike when confronted with matters beyond human genius and beyond human control.

It is fitting to close this reflection on prayer of petition with a petition: Father, we your children ask for the things we need, especially the things we cannot provide for ourselves — faith, hope, love, redemption, and life eternal with You. Put to shame those who try to shame our true faith in You. Instruct the ignorance of the intelligent, make them imitate Jesus in putting their intelligence at Your service and ours. Teach them to join us in praying for what we all need. Amen.

38. The Mystery of Mysteries

What is the greatest mystery with which you have to deal to make your life meaningful? Is there a solution to that mystery?

We all love a mystery. That is why *whodunits* are so popular. But if we all love a mystery, why do people neglect trying to solve the greatest mystery in their lives — the mystery of God? I think the neglect comes from people thinking that trying to solve the mystery of God is a hopeless task. Are they right? In what follows I hope to prove that they are wrong by showing that we are gradually solving the mystery of God.

Thousands of years ago men commonly believed that there were many gods. But God wanted men to know that He is the one God, so He began to reveal Himself. He chose the Jews to be the receivers and messengers of His revelation. Gradually, patiently, He made it clear to the Jews that He alone is God.

Almost two thousand years ago a certain pagan philosopher also believed there was only one God, and it was for that very reason that he felt sorry for God. For, he said, God alone has no companion like to Himself. He alone has to live alone.

What that pagan philosopher did not know is that God had already revealed that He is not alone. He had revealed and given to Mary His Divine eternal Son to become her human Son. And the Son in turn gave us the Holy Spirit, and so revealed that the Father and the Son are not alone. There are three persons in one God.

And in order that mothers and daughters may not seem to be left out of this mystery of God, let us recall that God Himself revealed that He made mankind in His image and likeness, "male and female he made them." We don't know exactly how we are like God, but one thing is certain: God is not alone. God is a family affair. God is love.

Over two thousand years ago that philosopher of philosophers, the great Aristotle, made a statement about God that would startle us today. He was writing about friendship. He said that the basis and foundation of friendship is a similarity and a kind of equality among the parties who would be friends. Thus, he said, there can be no friendship between man and God because they are so unequal.

Today we know that Aristotle was wrong. We know more than Aristotle, though he was one of the greatest geniuses of all time. God gave Aristotle a great brain, but He gave us a great revelation. Aristotle's knowledge of God came from his human mind, but ours comes from God's own mind.

It is not so much that Aristotle was wrong as that he has become wrong. Since Aristotle lived, God has become a man, become one of us. Jesus could now say to Aristotle: *What great inequality between God and man?* "Handle me, and see . . . flesh and bones" (Lk. 24:39). Not only that, but man now has the chance to become godlike by God's power — that is, by baptism. In fact, Jesus said almost what Aristotle said, except that He said it could all be changed by baptism: Jesus said that "no one can see the reign of God unless he is begotten from above. . . . no one can enter into God's kingdom without being begotten of water and Spirit" (Jn. 3:3, 5 NAT).

God is mystery, but we can enter into the mystery. God wants to be known, as a father wants to be known to his children and a bridegroom to his bride. He has begun to reveal to us the divine family mystery of the Trinity. He has given us His Son to share the life of the family of man. And His Son has invited us into the family of God. By pondering the Scriptures, receiving the Eucharist, and praying and meditating daily, we enter the mystery of God and are even made a part of it.

39. Love Yourself as Your Neighbor

To be a good Christian must you hate yourself? Is self-love or self-hatred the foundation of a sound Christian life?

A psychiatrist said he never had a patient with a good self-image. His patients were patients because they viewed themselves as disgusting.

Is this the ideal of Christianity — to hate yourself? Indeed it is not! It is a sickness and a corruption of Christianity. But does not Scripture — in fact, does not Jesus Himself — say, "If anyone comes to me and does not hate . . . his own life, he cannot be my disciple"? Yes, but Scripture also says elsewhere that the man who sins hates his own soul. Now if Scripture warns that sin is self-hatred, it is warning us against both sin and self-hatred. It is warning us against sin as self-hatred.

This poses a dilemma: Scripture seems to say in one place that you must not hate yourself and in another that you must hate yourself. How do we get to the bottom of this matter? I think we can do it by studying the Hebrew idiom in which the Scriptures were written. In Hebrew, the words *to hate* can be an emphatic way of saying *to love less*. For instance, God says: "I have loved Jacob and hated Esau" (Rom. 9:13). With this meaning in mind, let us go back to Jesus' words about self-hatred. Jesus said: "If anyone comes to me and does not hate his own father and mother and wife and children and brothers and sisters, yes, and even his own life, he cannot be my disciple" (Lk. 14:26). Now surely it is evident that to hate our parents and the rest of our family is against both the Ten Commandments and Jesus' own commandment of love. It is clear Jesus is really saying: Unless you love your parents and family and yourself less than Me, you can't be faithful to Me. If you don't love your health, your body, and your mortal life less

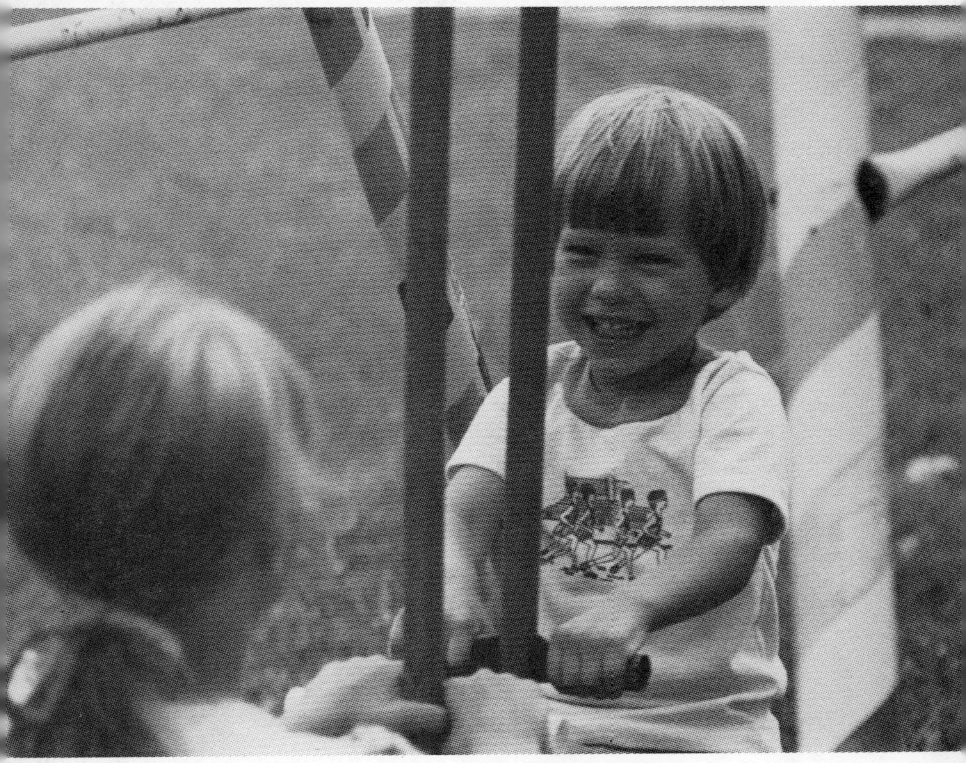

than Me, in a crisis you are going to choose those things in preference to Me, and at that point it becomes clear you were never My disciple.

Is it not evident Jesus is teaching us to love our real selves and to hate only our false selves? We should love our real selves more than we love our pleasure and our ease or we will destroy ourselves. We should love ourselves truly or we will not love our neighbor truly. We should love ourselves rightly, or we will not love our neighbor rightly. We should not be afraid of loving ourselves too much as long as we love ourselves rightly. What chance does our neighbor have of getting any love from us if we don't even have love to give ourselves? I've noticed that people who are too self-critical are also too critical of everyone else.

The secret of a healthy self-love is to see ourselves as God's own handiwork which He loves, and to love ourselves because He loves us. Christ said: "Love one another as I have loved you." Then why not be bold enough to say: "I want to love my neighbor and myself as Christ loves me"?

But, you may object, *I am a worthless sinner and God doesn't love sinners.* Well, dear sinner, listen to what St. Paul wrote to the Romans: "It is precisely in this that God proves his love for us: that while we were still sinners, Christ died for us" (Rom. 5:8 NAT).

There is no way out of it. We ought to love ourselves. We ought to love ourselves so much that we will want to rejoice in ourselves and celebrate ourselves and keep ourselves for God and for love, for sinlessness and selflessness, always self-loving but never self-centered.

40. Spiritual Monkey Children

Do you really know youself in the new creation you have become? Or have you gradually forgotten your true identity in Christ Jesus?

Not long ago reports out of Burundi described how a child of six was discovered climbing about the jungle with a troop of monkeys. He could not talk; he grunted and chattered. He resisted wearing clothes, ate only fruits and vegetables, and uttered threatening monkey cries. He was dubbed the monkey child, though there is a conflicting report that he was not raised by monkeys but is simply a retarded child.

According to the original report, this child does not know how to be human and does not even know that he is human because from the age of two to six he was raised by monkeys. This report bears a striking resemblance to the many cases of what we might call spiritual monkey children. Spiritual monkey children are people who were reborn in Christ, but got so involved in things outside of Christ they forgot their new identity in Him. St. James describes the process when he writes: "If anyone is a hearer of the word and not a doer, he is like a man who observes his natural face in a mirror; for he observes himself and goes away and at once forgets what he looks like" (James 1:23 - 24).

The process of becoming spiritual monkey children begins when believers start to forget who Jesus Christ is. They forget that He is not just another human being but a new creation, the new Adam, the "last Adam" (1 Cor. 15:45), the first immortal man. They forget that He is not just a new creation, but the uncreated, the eternal Son of God sent by the Father to become a man in order to save all men.

Once they start neglecting Jesus, they forget their new birth in Him through baptism. Once they begin to forget they have been "born anew" by "water and the Spirit" (Jn. 3:3, 5), they start to lose their belief that they are really "God's children now" as St. John teaches (1 Jn. 3:2). Once they start disbelieving they are God's children they begin to ignore Paul's exhortation to "be immitators of God, as beloved children," and "walk in love, as Christ loved us" (Eph. 5:1 - 2). Once they lose the impulse to imitate God and His Son Jesus Christ they begin neglecting Mass and Communion, Scriptural reading and prayer. By now they are becoming spiritually deaf, so that they no longer even hear the Holy Spirit giving witness to their spirits that they are the children of God (Rom. 8:16). At this point they are well on the way to becoming spiritual monkey children, no longer able to live as children of God or even remember that they are children of God.

Pope Paul spoke of baptismal rebirth and of the danger of rearing what I am calling spiritual monkey children. He said baptism gives us rebirth in Christ, a share in His life, and a destiny of eternal happiness if we are faithful. Then he adds, and I quote: "We should meditate more on this good fortune . . . we must often observe that Christians are not always aware of being Christians. . . . Think . . . of the . . . feeble awareness a child has of his election to the supernatural religious order. Catholic pedagogy should aim at once at creating in the child, in the boy, in the youth, this . . . adverting to being a Christian. A boy may have this awareness, as he is aware . . . of being a member of one tribe rather than another, or of being a member of a people, a nation, a race. With all the more reason should we cultivate in the adolescent awareness of his religion, and especially the Catholic religion, which confers on the youthful conscience itself the sense of communion with God, with Christ, with the saints, with the dead, with the living Church . . . (and) a decisive moral and social orientation."

We should refuse to be spiritual monkey children, and refuse to raise them. We should read about Jesus in the Scriptures, pray to Jesus, worship Jesus and imitate Jesus, and teach our children to do the same. We should be children of God now and always and forever.

41. Little Helps to Love

Is it possible to name some practices that help love to grow in your life? Is it useful to draw up a list of helps to love?

We are more often told to love than told how to grow in love. Yet we know that it helps to go about a thing rightly. The farmer who wants to grow a crop of wheat has to know how to do it. He needs to know what kind of seed to buy and when to plant it, and how to prepare the soil and whether it needs fertilizer. With this in mind, let us compare growing a crop of wheat with growing the crop of love.

To begin with, we need the seeds of love. Where do we get them? The seeds of love spring into being in our hearts whenever we perceive the true, the good, and the beautiful. A person with qualities of truth, goodness, and beauty awakens spontaneous love in us. Therefore, our first little help to love can be stated thus: Produce many seeds of love by cultivating the habit of looking for the good in others.

When the farmer has gotten his supply of seeds he needs suitable soil in which to plant them. Similarly, the truth, goodness and beauty which we see in others must be given the chance to penetrate deep into our hearts. The only suitable soil for the seeds of love is a meditative and recollected heart. I have never met anyone more loving than cloistered contemplative sisters, or anyone less likely to be loving than the busied person. Overly busy people are shallow and poor lovers. We should avoid their fault and be like Mary, the Mother of Jesus. She found time to pray and ponder her experiences in her heart. Our second practice, then, is: We must build some repose into our lives.

Now the trouble is, repose doesn't just happen by willing it. We need to plan daily periods of quiet and meditation. Unless we day-by-day give priority to the important things and daily

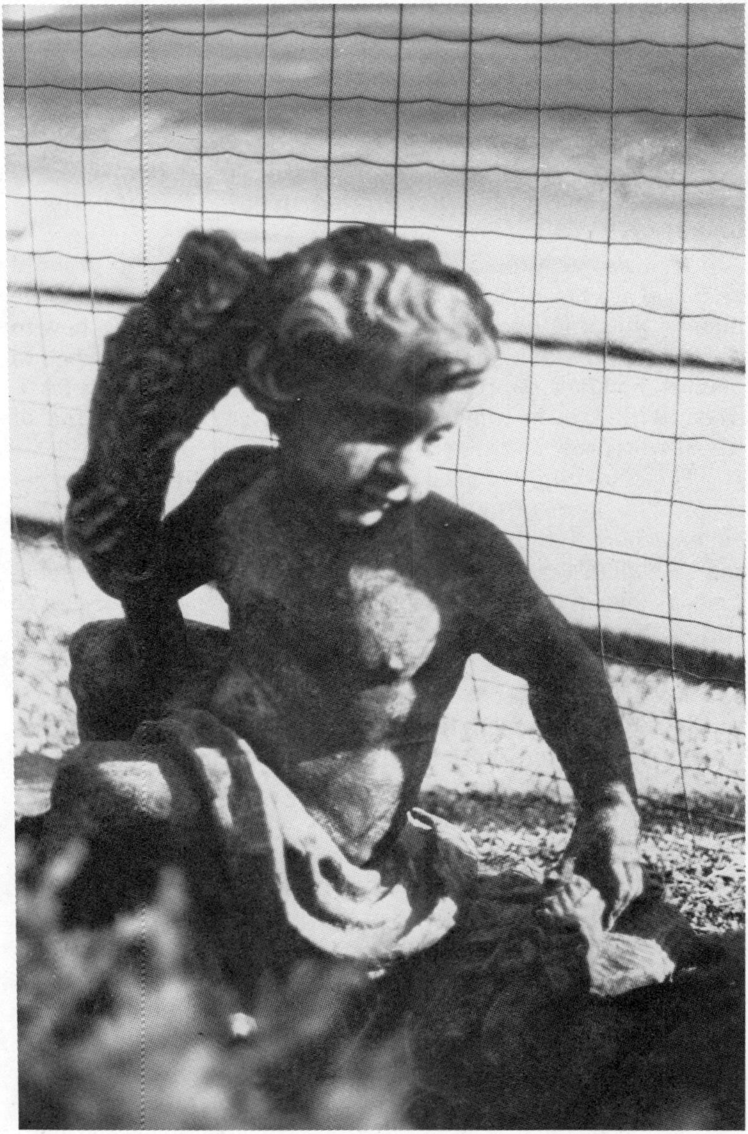

weed out the unimportant things, the weeds of disorder will stifle the crop of love in our lives. But balance is needed here, for too much planning makes our lives harsh and unyielding. It leads to frequent frustration, and that leads to bursts of impatience, and impatience is a great enemy of love. So our third practice is: We need to plan our day to keep it ordered, uncluttered, and flexible.

Besides choosing good seed and preparing the soil, farmers have other little secrets for producing better crops. Here are some other secrets for growing the crop of love. First, love feeds very much on love memories, so we need to relive often the earlier love experiences of our lives. Better still, we remember together. That's what anniversaries are all about. For instance, the Last Supper was so memorable for Jesus and His followers that we have been reliving it with Him ever since.

Second, we should avoid being overly self-sufficient. It is a delusion. We need one another. We are wise to say it.

Third, when we hurt others we should admit our fault as soon as we can bring ourselves to it. Denial of our faults can hurt love more than the faults.

Fourth, we should make some extra little sacrifice for love every day. It says to someone, "I love you." After all, love is a gift-giving, and in the end the only real gift we can give is ourselves, and self-sacrifice is always the giving of self.

Fifth, we should resolve to keep the Sixth Commandment faithfully. Carnal love is a true part of love, but the abuse of it destroys all love.

Sixth, we ought to realize that love is not so much a giving to others, as a living for others. The little helps to love already mentioned are ways of living for others. Therefore, they are not only helps to love; they are helps to happiness and to the discovery of God, our final beatitude.

42. Improving Our Prayer of Petition

Can prayer of petition fail you? Is there anything you can do to improve your prayer of petition and avoid bitter disappointments and a loss of trust in God?

I suppose we have all had disappointing experiences with prayer of petition. That is not necessarily bad. There is an old axiom, *Live and learn.* The important thing is: Did we learn? Did we meditate and find out why our prayer was not answered? Did we learn how to ask more wisely and to live in a more mature and responsible relationship with God? If so, our experience was one of growth, and that growth itself was probably God's answer to our prayer.

There are certain defects we can fall into in our prayer of petition. The first is to have a wrong world view underlying our prayer of petition. I can illustrate this defect with model cities. In medieval Europe the heart and center of a city was its house of God, its cathedral. Even from a distance the cathedral was seen as the focal point of the city, the guiding landmark for the approaching traveler. This city plan also served as a model for the life pattern of each medieval citizen. God was to be the guiding center of their lives too.

Now contrast the medieval city with a modern one. In the modern city it is usually some house of man, some towering business center, which is the focal point of the city. In such a city one has to search for a house of God.

In our own minds too we can set up these man-centered models of life, and they can be the cause of failed prayer of petition. People with these man-centered and self-centered models ask God to arrange their lives around themselves as the center instead of asking Him to arrange their lives around Him as the center. Unthinkingly, they demote God to the role of a servant in their lives and in their very prayer. For instance, they pray for riches when God knows that because of their weak love for Him they would forget Him completely if they were given the wealth that they ask. God will not answer such self-centered prayer.

Before we ask God to change some major factor in our lives or the lives of others, we should carefully consider whether we are asking for a curse instead of a blessing. In the Middle Ages when the master artists painted those great murals, they were assisted by apprentices. The masters would do the great and intricate parts of their painting. Then they might entrust to an apprentice the task of filling in the lesser details. For me, God is the great Master Painter, the Lord of History, and by prayer of petition we fill in the lesser details. We are the masterpieces He is creating day by day. When I pray for something, how careful I try to be not to ruin His work by asking for something out of place! It would be like spattering paint on Michelangelo's murals in the Sistine Chapel!

Just yesterday I was talking to a young mother with a child at home who has been almost helpless from birth. This mother never felt impelled to pray for a miracle. She seems to sense a deeper divine purpose in this matter. She has received much advice, but she feels an inner wisdom of her own as great as that of people twice her age. Her Catholic faith has given her confidence in God, and composure in bearing her own and her child's suffering.

The lesson is this: Before we make a serious request of God, we should think over our own life and consult our own heart to see if what we are about to ask really suits us and really harmonizes with God's evident purpose in our lives. If our request meets this test, let us ask, and ask with faith that we will receive.

43. The Lamb Who Is Shepherd

Why do the Scriptures call Jesus both a Lamb and a Shepherd? What meaning does this dual role of Jesus have for us?

The Book of Revelation calls Jesus "the Lamb," but Jesus likened Himself to the Shepherd who cares for the lambs. Now how could Jesus be both a lamb led by a shepherd, and a Shepherd who leads all the lambs? If He is a Lamb, who leads Him?

A reflection on these questions promises to give us a deeper understanding of Jesus our Good Shepherd, and of what He expects from us. In the Old Testament, God appointed priests, prophets and kings to shepherd His people. Often He was bitter and angry with them because they were false shepherds. So God made a great promise. He said: "I myself will gather the remnant of my flock" (Jer. 23:3 NAT). In other words, God Himself promised to be our Shepherd. We know that promise was fulfilled in His Son Jesus Christ who said: "I am the Good Shepherd."

How does this Shepherd lead us? Well, He certainly does not take refuge in that old axiom: "Don't do as I do; do as I say." No, Jesus could say "I am the way" because He lived the way we ought to live, and went the way we ought to go to God. Jesus led the way by living it. Then who was His Shepherd? Clearly, the Father and Lord of us all. That is why Jesus says in the Gospel of John: "When you lift up the Son of Man you will come to realize that I AM and that I do nothing by myself. I say only what the Father has taught me. . . . I did not come of my own will; it was he who sent me" (Jn. 8:28, 42 NAT).

This, then, is the kind of Shepherd we have. He instructs us more by what He does than by what He says. Jesus teaches us obedience by being obedient; He teaches us love by loving, and service by dying; He teaches us giving by giving all He had: His Father and Mother, His friends, His very self.

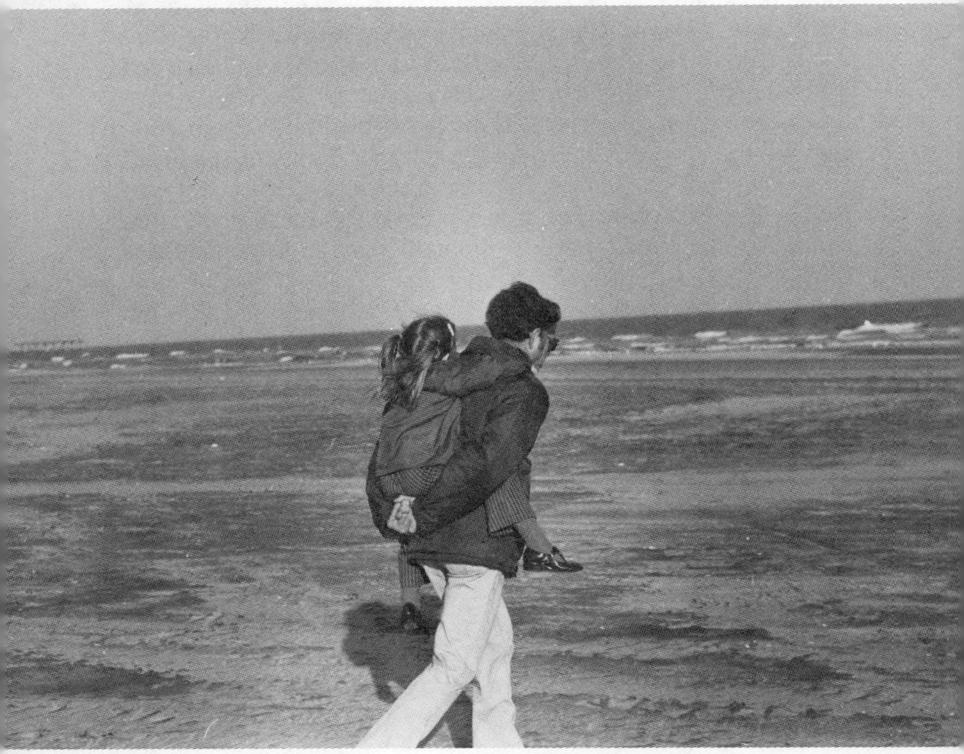

Let us look at the role of a shepherd and of a sheep, and see how Jesus fulfills both roles. The role of a shepherd is to guide his sheep to pasture and to teach them how to live in security — to be their leader and protector. Now we know that Jesus did all these things for us. He guides us to eternal life; He teaches us the way to act; He leads us by going ahead Himself, and He protects us always.

Jesus was also like the sheep which we are to be. Now a sheep provides clothing and food for his shepherd, for he provides his wool for clothing; and sometimes he provides his flesh for food — for sometimes the sheep must die for the shepherd. But marvelously, it is our Shepherd who clothes us, as St. Paul says: "Put on Christ." It is our Shepherd who feeds us. Jesus said: "He who eats my flesh and drinks my blood has eternal life," for His flesh alone is immortal.

And in doing all of this Jesus has given us an example so that we may be both sheep and shepherds. Think of the priest as shepherd of his people; but remember also that every parent is shepherd of his children, and everyone who gives good example shepherds others by himself living in the likeness of Christ.

So we are called like Jesus Himself to be always sheep following Him, but in some ways shepherds leading with Him.

O Lord Jesus, you are our Shepherd. O Good Shepherd, we shall not want. At the altar table you set up for us, how good is the food!

44. Woman of Women

Do you think of Mary the Mother of Jesus as a prophetess? Why not share the blessing of helping to fulfill the biblical prophecy which she made?

When I began my studies for the priesthood some years

ago I used to recite the Little Office of the Blessed Virgin Mary. I would begin with that lovely little prayer: "How to praise thee O sacred Virgin, I have no idea!" I wasn't aware at the time that I was dealing with the difficulty of fulfilling Mary's great biblical prophecy, for Mary the prophetess said: "Behold, henceforth all generations will call me blessed" (Lk. 1:48).

Before ever Mary existed God prophesied concerning her in the Book of Genesis. He said to the serpent: "I will put enmity between you and the woman and between your seed and her seed; he shall bruise your head" (3:15).

Mary is also prefigured in many Old Testament women: in the fruitfulness of Eve — but not in her unfaithfulness; in the loveliness of Rachel; in the sterility of Hannah, a sterility which was overcome by the power of God and led Hannah to sing her song of praise as you, Mary, would sing yours with such beauty. And you were prefigured, Mary, in Esther the lovely Queen whose intercession with the great king saved her whole people. And so Dante in writing his *Divine Comedy,* mindful of your powerful intercession with God wrote: "So mighty art thou, lady, and so great, that anyone who desires grace and does not come to you for help is trying to have his prayer fly without wings!"

And the Song of Songs speaks of you where the bridegroom calls his fair bride and says: "As a lily among thorns, so is my beloved among women." And your glory, Mary, is found in that Old Testament Psalm 45 where God says: "Hear, O daughter, and see; turn your ear, forget your people and your father's house. So shall the king desire your beauty; for he is your Lord and you must worship him. . . . All glorious is the king's daughter as she enters. . . . The place of your fathers your sons shall have; you shall make them princes through all the land . . . therefore shall nations praise you forever and ever" (Ps. 45:1 - 18 NAT). O Mary, you must have seen yourself in this prophecy! For as you entered history you were already the Immaculate Conception, full of beauty! As Christ is the perfect Redeemer, you are the perfectly redeemed one. And you entered history and you believed in Christ, and you had to "forget" your people by going beyond their faith because they wanted to anathematize you for your faith, for John tells us that the Jews had "agreed among themselves that anyone who acknowledged Jesus as Messiah would be put out of the synagogue" (Jn. 9:22 NAT).

And the psalm says: "The place of your fathers your sons shall have; you shall make them princes through all the land." And we believe, O Mary, we believe that we are your sons. We believe that because we share the life of Jesus. He is the head and we the members. Because we are one with the life of Jesus who is your Son, we are your children. And so, Mary, we share your nobility; we are the princes of eternal life in God. And so forever we will sing your praise and say: "Hail, full of grace . . . blessed are you among women. Blessed is the fruit of your womb, Jesus!"

45. The Mystery of Happiness

Have you ever noticed strange patterns in human happiness? Have you ever noticed people happy whom you would expect to be unhappy and vice versa? What is the mystery of happiness?

We human beings are a strange breed. When emptiest we are the fullest, and when fullest the emptiest. Men have climbed to the top of their profession — and in that instant found it empty, a blind alley — and walked away. Other men have lost everything, and in that instant found happiness.

We are a strange breed. Have you ever seen a fully satisfied man? I have not! Self-satisfied, yes, but satisfied, never! I've seen contented cows, but not fully contented men. The closest to a satisfied man is one who is satisfied by anticipation. It's not what he possesses and has accomplished that counts, but what he hopes to possess and accomplish.

Man lives in hope, and he lives in action, moving him toward his hope. There is a philosophy that says, "It's the action and go-go that counts." This is false. As sound philosophers say: "Everything that acts, acts for a purpose." And we too act for a purpose and a final goal.

What is the goal? Is it gold? A golden girl? A golden hour in the sun? All these are good, but they contain only a taste of goodness, not satiety. Like a broken shard of glass reflecting fragments of beauty beyond itself, these things reflect a taste of the Divine. A bridegroom holds his beloved in his arms, and it only awakens his hunger for love; it does not satiate it. Recognize the mystery and ponder it.

The mystery of creation is that God the Creator has left the scent and the spoor of Himself upon all the parts and pathways of Creation. And in anything where one does not pick up this scent and this spoor and get this taste, there is no life for him. And so the psalmist says: "O God, you are my God whom I seek. For you my soul thirsts, you my flesh desires as an arid and parched land without water."

We find God in His creation, but we find Him more in silence than in sound; more in poverty than in riches; more in failure than in success; more in those things that are open and spacious and leave room for Him than in those things that crowd our flighty hearts with their self-importance.

Without God, life is empty. It is a story without an ending, a wedding without a wedding couch, a success without significance, a journey without a destination, a ship without a harbor, a haunting desire never identified.

I tried to capture this mystery of man and of the Christian in verse entitled STRANGE BREED:

> I belong to a strange breed of men.
> Twice born, already buried once,
> We die now no more.
> With strong feet, tramping glad

These earthly paths, laughing tear-stained
In exile, for we are marching home.

We outshout wanton cry of freedom
With strong shout: Hail King of kings and Lord of lords!
We bow, too, with humble supplication
And love inestimable, to a Queen:

Men talk much useless talk,
But we learn morning silence with open mouth
Before God's mouth, to catch
His Word in ours.
His Word lights us, strange breed of men,
On our unearthly journey,
For we are marching home.

46. What's It All About, Lord?

What is the fundamental difference between the times of our despair and the times of our fullness? What gives life a sense of meaning?

How often have men stared into the dying embers of a fire, and seen in them a reflection of their own lives — lives passing them by, ending cold and without purpose or meaning?

But how many men, too, have known times when they were unabashedly happy — ashamed to be so happy when so many others were suffering so much so continuously? Have there not been those times in our lives when we found so much joy and meaning in life that the question of understanding life never arose because the solution preceded the question?

What was the difference between those two states, the one of despair and the other of fullness? If we can answer that question we will have satisfied a deep hunger for understanding. More important we will have an answer to guide our future.

Let us look for that guiding principle by asking a simple question: What is the fundamental difference between the times of our despair and the times of our fullness? Is there one factor which is always present in times of fullness and never present in times of despair?

I have known well-to-do people who were very unhappy and poor people who were very happy. I have known healthy people who were unhappy and sick people who were happy. I have known famous people who were unhappy and unknowns who were happy. Clearly, then, the heart of happiness does not lie with riches, health or fame. Where does it lie?

My mother told me of the days just after she married my father. They were so poor they had to await payday to buy the necessities of life. And yet she was deliriously happy. She had only one thing: love. And yet her joy was almost full.

And I recall the days when I took my first vows in religion. I was given a book of prayer and a crucifix and a vow of poverty. And with it I found joy.

Where then is the meaning of life centered? It is centered in love. Why is it that love and its fullness so often vanish and the emptiness returns? God's word gives us the answer. We find the Lord saying that the fires we thought would burn forever were only fires of flesh that burn away; the bottles into which we put the meaning of our lives were untrustworthy. They broke and meaning drained away. But God says in Christ: "If anyone thirsts let him come to me. . . . Scripture has it: From within him rivers of living waters shall flow" (Jn. 7:37 - 38 NAT).

Only when our loves are centered in God do they burn with the elemental Fire that never goes out. Only then are we assured that our love will never pass away — that we have reached eternal meaning in our lives.

47. Making Decisions in the Lord

When faced with decisions how can we make good ones? How can we discern the course that best pleases the Lord?

The Acts of the Apostles tell us how Paul set out with fire in his eye to arrest and jail Christians. Because of his cocksure subjectivity that he was doing right, he went off and did harm to the Lord. By the grace of God the Lord appeared to him and showed him his error, and Paul said: "Lord, what do you want me to do?" And the Lord told him how to find out.

How can we avoid Paul's error of attacking God's purposes in the name of God? How can we learn what God wants us to do? Just as these problems arose in the life of Paul, the answers come to us from Paul. Paul gives us both the method and the principles for avoiding this cocksure subjectivism.

The method is to remember that we have to make all our decisions within the limits of the teaching of Revelation and the Church.

The principles for living out this method are also given us by Paul: First, the individual Catholic subjects himself to the institutional Church in all things except sin. Paul wrote: "Let every person be subject to the governing authorities. For there is no authority except from God, and those that exist have been instituted by God" (Rom. 13:1).

Second, the individual Catholic must form, nourish, and adjust his belief and conduct in all things to the faith and morals taught by the Church. The reason is that the Revelation in Jesus Christ was given once and for all, and it is handed on to us by the Church alone in a fully trustworthy fashion. St. Paul wrote to the Galatians: "I am amazed that you . . . are going over to another gospel. But there is no other. For even if we, or an angel from heaven, should preach to you a gospel not

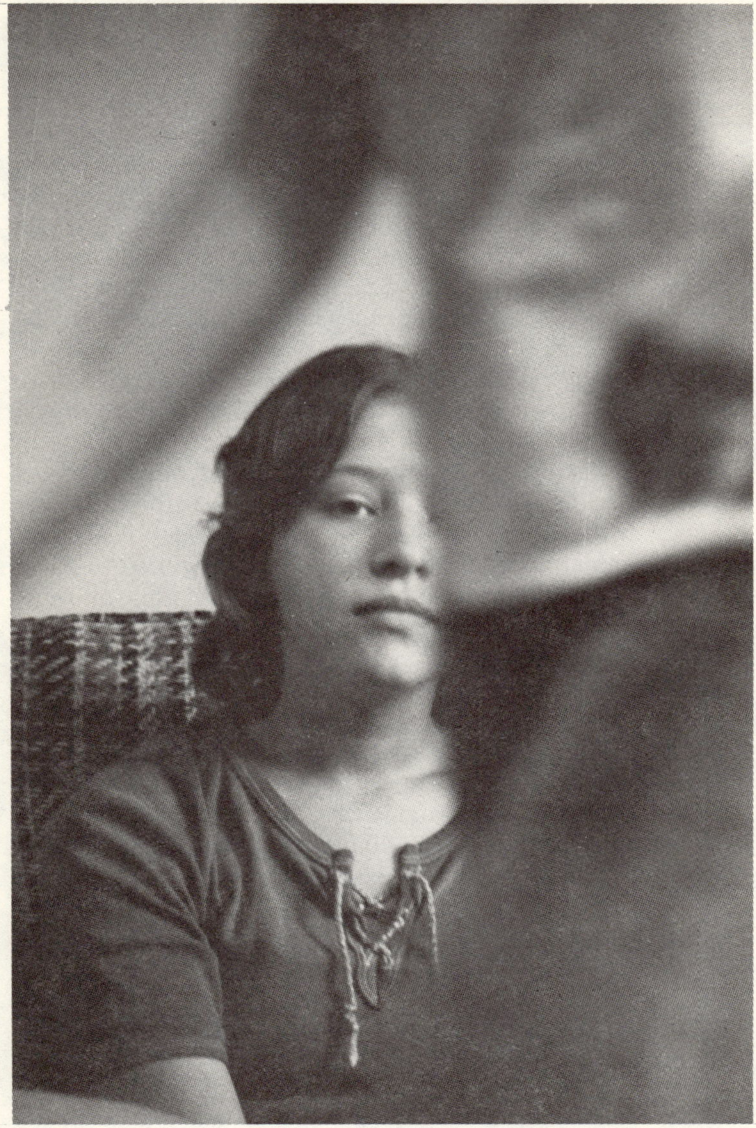

in accord with the one we delivered to you, let a curse be upon him" (Gal. 1:6 - 8 NAT).

Third, even charismatic and inspirational impulses must obey these same principles, as Paul makes clear. The reason is that there is only one Spirit and He guides both the Church and the members, and does not contradict Himself and divide the Church. Paul warns the Corinthians that Satan sometimes puts on the guise of an "angel of light" to deceive and divide us — as he tricked Eve.

Let us say, then, that someone is faced with a decision and has several courses of conduct open. Which does God want him to adopt? I propose three norms to help him find out: First, an objective norm; which course looks best as judged by law and duty?

The second norm is an interior norm, a subjective one: As he considers the several courses, which course does he find brings him the most peace and joy? Notice, I say peace and joy, not contentment at the thought of escaping suffering and burdens. Peace and joy can be found even in suffering, as Jesus said. Peace and joy are the fruits of love and the Holy Spirit.

The third norm is both objective and subjective: Which course is most harmonious with the whole course of his life, especially in its inner meaning and holiness?

When he finds the one course that satisfies his responsibilities, gives him a sense of peace and joy, and harmonizes with the spiritual meaning of his whole life, he has pretty surely found what the Lord is calling him to do. He has only to decide in the Lord to go ahead and do it!

PART 6

48. The Ever-Human Jesus

Do we so drive home our faith in the Divinity of Jesus that we lose contact with His humanity? What can we do to correct this serious error?

We Christians, and especially we Catholics, have so zealously and devotedly guarded our faith in the Divinity of Jesus Christ for two thousand years that we have sometimes endangered the fullness of our understanding that Jesus is as human as — and more human than — you and I; for He is human in its perfectibility.

How can we grasp more fully the humanness of Jesus? Since knowledge of Jesus is a gift, let us first pray to the Father for that gift:

> O Father in heaven, your only Son told us expressly that no one knows Him except You, the Father, and that no one can come to Him unless You draw him. And so we pray that You may draw us still more to Jesus and reveal Him to us in His humanity and His Divinity. Amen.

Now to the mystery of Jesus: The people who knew Jesus during His mortal life could hardly doubt His humanity. Think of the Apostles eating, drinking and talking with Him every day — seeing Him getting so tired that He would fall asleep and stay asleep in a boat in a terrible storm — seeing Him do all the things that human beings do and never for a moment doubting that He was as human as they.

If we ask James and John, who were taken into the special confidence of Jesus, whether He was as human as we are, they might say to us: "If it is human to be tempted, He was surely as human as we. We never saw a man more tempted than He, in His agony in the garden; and if it is human to have feelings and to love and to fear, we never saw one more human than He. We never saw a love greater than His as He expressed it at the Last Supper. We never saw a fear greater than His in the agony, when His sweat became as drops of blood."

And if we asked Mary Magdalen our question, she might say: "If it is human to love, I assure you I never saw a more loving man. Other men taught me lust, but He taught me a virginal love which I thought was beyond me. I have known many people who loved everything good, but He also loved everyone bad and wanted nothing more than to share His goodness with them."

And Martha, Lazarus's sister, might have said to us: "If it is human to seek God's help in our limited abilities and our great needs, then I never knew one more human than Jesus. When my brother died He cried with loud shouts and great tears to God and He was heard, and my brother rose!"

And Joseph might say: "Would you like to know my experience of how human He is? I taught Him His trade and mine. I saw Him learn like other little boys and girls. I saw that it was sometimes hard for Him to obey me when He had opinions of His own."

And Mary might say to us: "Human? I felt His little body stirring in my womb before He was born and I nursed Him at my breast and I fed Him daily with the meals I cooked for Him. He was so human it was hard to know He was more. And yet, He was more than human, as all who believe in Him know. It was only by meditation and prayer and pondering on Scripture that I could come to know this; so human was He that I had to struggle to have the fullness of faith in His Divinity as Son of God."

The letter to the Hebrews says: "In the days of his flesh, Jesus offered up prayers and supplications with loud cries and tears to God . . . and he was heard for his godly fear. Although he was a Son, he learned obedience through what he suffered" (Heb. 5:7 - 8).

The best way to learn the mystery of Jesus is to live in His likeness. For as we struggle to be like Him, we more and more taste the mystery of the God-man. This is as He promised: "If you continue in my word, you are truly my disciples and you will know the truth. . . . I am . . . the truth" (Jn. 8:31; 14:6).

49. Dereliction

Have you ever felt altogether abandoned and alone? What is the secret of survival amid the despair of abandonment?

In the days of His passion Jesus was delivered into the hands of sinners as though He were a sinner receiving His just deserts. But the wild acts of men working their will upon Him is not what makes the passion of Jesus so much worse than anything that had gone before in His life. Long before the passion He was insulted by men and persecuted by them and even called a madman. At Nazareth they tried to throw Him off a cliff. He had to make good His own escape. When He promised the Eucharist He knew rejection. His followers deserted Him in droves. What distinguishes the passion from His earlier sufferings is not that men persecuted Jesus, but that God abandoned Him. That is what explains His terror and grief in the agony. Jesus' life had been at stake before, but He had no such fear before, for up until now Jesus could always say that "he

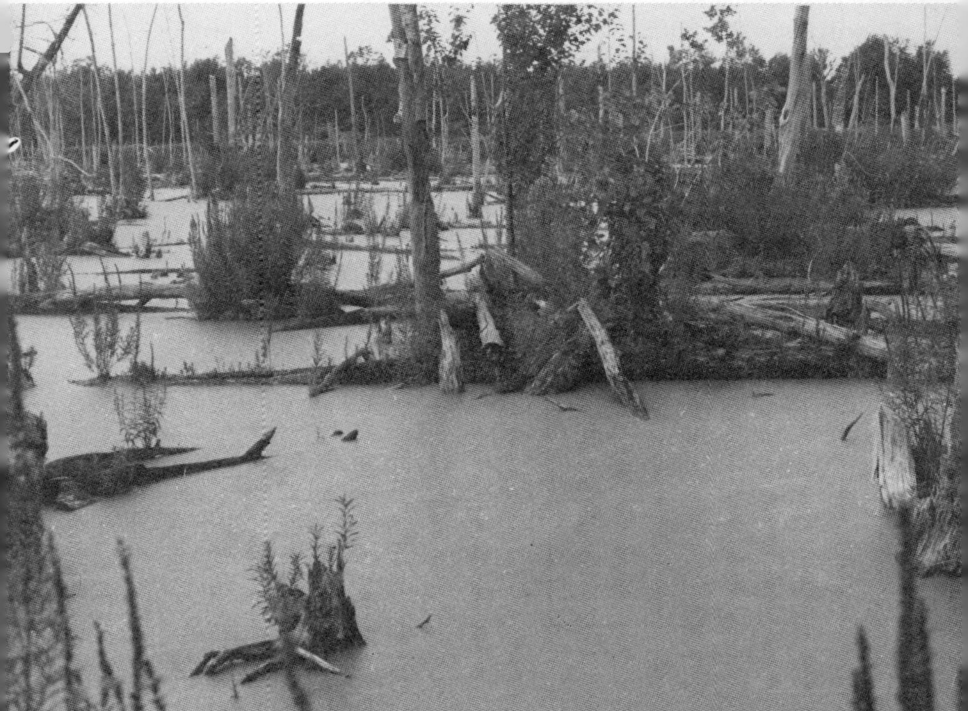

who sent me is with me; he has not left me alone . . ." (Jn. 8:29). But now terror almost overwhelmed Him. Now He had to cry: "My God, my God, why hast thou forsaken me?" (Mt. 27:46). The terror of the passion is that He was betrayed from without and abandoned from within.

The scandal of the passion is that Jesus experienced not only the perfidy of men but dereliction by God. Until now, though His exterior fate might be indistinguishable from sinners, His interior experience was that of the Saint of saints. But now, neither within nor without does His experience distinguish Him from the sinner. In fact, I would conjecture that within He was more abandoned than the sinner. For I cannot believe that God does not interiorly visit the dying sinner to offer him salvation. We know for a fact that many a sinner has died in the consolation of God. And we know that some martyrs — St. Lawrence for one — have died at the hands of their enemies without the horror and fear that Jesus experienced because all the while they have experienced the consolation of God.

This is a shocking scandal — that we cannot tell from without, and Jesus cannot tell from within, that God has not abandoned Him. So deep and terrible is the mystery of our salvation.

When an animal is mortally wounded, he withdraws into a cave to hover between life and death until one or the other claims him. When a man's soul is terribly wounded, he tends to withdraw into the cave of his own deeper self to survive and endure. But even before he withdraws from his surroundings psychologically, his friends only too often withdraw from him physically, as happened to Jesus, and as the Psalms foretold: "My friends and companions stand aloof from my plague, and my kinsmen stand afar off" (Ps. 38:11). This withdrawal insulates and isolates, and that is very dangerous. That is too much like selfishness — the act by which we insulate and isolate ourselves from the lives of others. Mourning must not be allowed to degenerate into melancholia, or the mourner may never come out of himself again.

Yet the motives of mourning and selfishness differ. The motive of selfishness is not to have to give. The motive of the withdrawal into self in dereliction is to commune with the self because there is none other left with which to commune, not even God — to ponder the terror and the meaning.

And yet, here lurks the crisis unsuspected. Should we withdraw from others when they withdraw from us? Should we stop speaking to God when He does not answer?

Jesus did not stop. He did not turn from the Father but kept repeating: "Father . . . remove this cup from me" (Mk. 14:36). He did not turn from His persecutors but kept saying: "Father, forgive them" (Lk. 23:34). He did not stop believing in the Father. He did not stop trusting Him. "Father," He said, "into thy hands I commend my spirit" (Lk. 23:46).

Here lies insight into the mystery of suffering. Suffering of dereliction calls for the ultimate renunciation of isolation. It burns away the insulation. It strips the soul naked of all concealments. It disposes it for union. "And I," Jesus once said, "when I am lifted up from earth, will draw all men to myself" (Jn. 12:32). And so it has happened to Him, and through Him it will happen to us.

50. Saint Joseph and Fatherhood

Is a father no more than the one who makes a woman a mother and who makes paychecks appear regularly in the home? How does Joseph clarify the nature of fatherhood?

In America today many wives are work widows because of the encroaching cultural norm that all a father and husband really has to do is appear weekly with his paycheck. The result is that many of our children are virtually without a father. The children are "work orphans."

What is the role of a father? Certainly his role is not solely physical generation. If it were, St. Joseph would have no right at all to be called a father, for his Son was not his by an act of generation on Joseph's part, but by a gift from God through Mary.

I think the world has never yet appreciated the fatherhood of Joseph because it has yet to understand what a father is. Joseph is a new Abraham who begot Christ in faith. When Abraham was too old to beget a child according to the ordinary laws of nature, he was given power to be a father. But Joseph was given a new power to be a father before he lost the natural power to generate a child, and he never employed that natural power at all. He was called to be a father not according to the law of nature, but according to the laws of spirit and faith.

Even the *Wall Street Journal* has lamented the reduction of fatherhood to one act of generation plus a regular paycheck. It decried the plight of the "work widow" produced by the husband who marries the company for which he works. After that the husband allows his wife to claim nothing of him but his paycheck and his bed. Since this caricature of fatherhood won't do, what is the true role of a father?

Modern psychology has done a great deal to illuminate the

role of a father. Let me bring out by a simple example what it teaches. If I say to you, "Build me a table," you may go off and build me one or you may ask, "What size, what shape, what material?" If you are a caveman you would also have to ask, "What is a table?" In other words, to make a table you need a pattern.

Now what is the pattern for personhood? We have heard stories of babies who lost their parents and were reared by animals — by apes and wolves. But one thing we know: an ape cannot rear a human being except to be an animal.

When an infant is brought into the world he or she cannot grow up without living with a living pattern for personhood day in and day out. And if the pattern fails him or her, that child will fail to grow up. The study of psychology vouches for this. Unless an adult male and female are on the scene the infant is grossly handicapped in personal growth. Each child needs both parents on the scene, but above all a boy needs a father and a girl needs a mother.

This reflection helps us to see how meaningfully Joseph was a father. He was the masculine pattern for personhood for the Son of God born into this world. And if we love Christ for the way He is, we owe our gratitude not only to God the Father and to Mary, but also to Joseph.

Anna Freud has done a clinical study of the difference in the role of a mother and a father. She found that a father is not merely an "assistant mother." She found one fundamental difference in the psychological roles of mother and father. When a child manifests a need the mother inclines to provide *instant gratification*. The father inclines to teach the need of a *delay in gratification*. In other words, the father introduces *discipline*. He introduces the reasoned awareness that not every human desire is to be immediately and spontaneously fulfilled.

Both observation and the Bible verify this difference in roles. The Letter to the Hebrews says, "The Lord disciplines him whom he loves and chastises every son whom he receives. . . . God is treating you as sons, for what son is there whom his

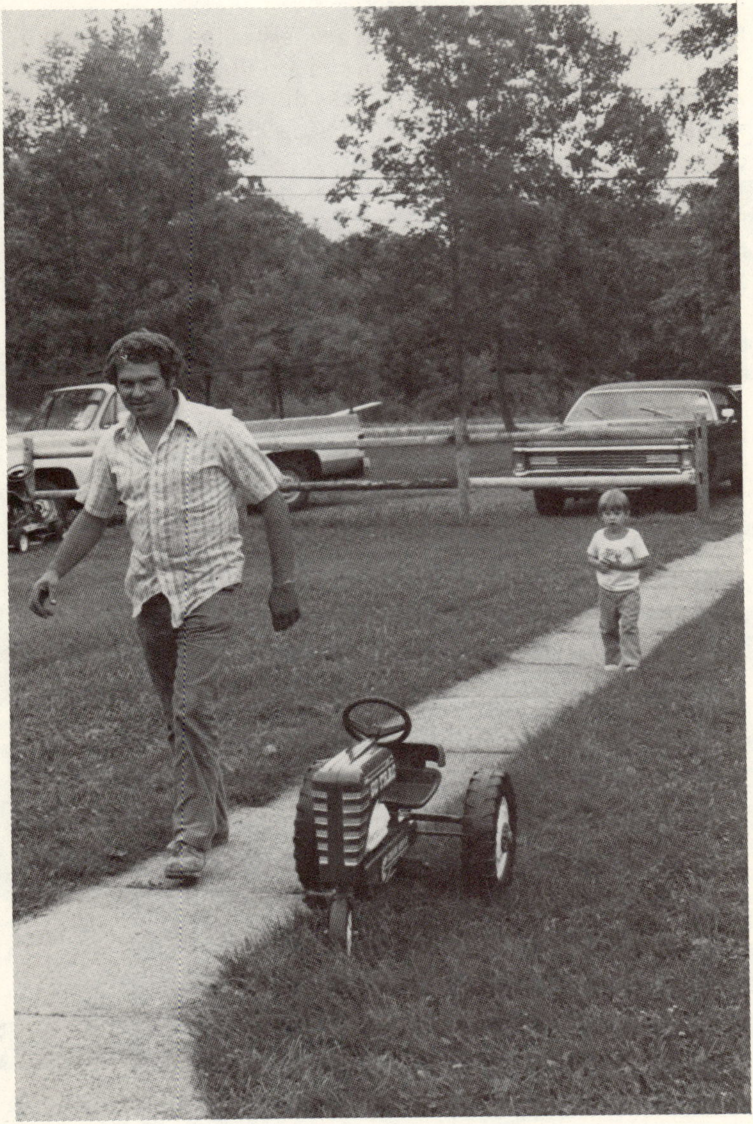

father does not discipline? If you are left without discipline in which all have participated, then you are illegitimate children and not sons" (Heb. 12:6 - 8). Unless the father introduces this role of discipline into the child's life, the child may prove to be undisciplined for life.

The father's disciplinary role has been rendered very difficult by a culture that translates freedom into license. There is a lack of discipline in almost every phase of American life, and the role of fatherhood is more often caricatured than portrayed respectfully in our literature and our media. One of the few TV programs that has ever portrayed a father as an admirable character was the series entitled *Bonanza*. It became popular around the world. The world is hungry for fathers, but I want to point out something ominous. In *Bonanza* there is no woman — no mother in the home. In our society can a man be a successful father only when he does not have the competition of a mother?

Let us honor Joseph as a man who lived with his wife and child, but lived out his fatherly responsibilities as the gospels show. The gospels show him as a man who would have renounced Mary rather than break God's law. He was a just and disciplined husband and father. The men and fathers of today need God the Father, St. Joseph, and their Son, Jesus, for their models to restore a civilization corrupted by lack of discipline.

51. Mercy We Can Count On

How can we deepen our confidence in God's mercy? What are the signs we have opened ourselves to His mercy?

If we are going to talk about God's mercy, the best place to start is in the storeroom of our own experiences. We have all experienced it, and I, as a priest, am no exception. Without his mercy I could not have been called, I could not have been forgiven, or made worthy, or kept faithful. The Letter to the Hebrews says: "Every high priest . . . can deal gently with the ignorant and wayward, since he himself is beset with weakness. Because of this he is bound to offer sacrifice for his own sins as well as those of the people" (Heb. 5:1 - 3).

We all need God's mercy because we all have needs we cannot supply ourselves. First of all, we need forgiveness for our sins and healing of our sinfulness, which is ever threatening us. Furthermore, we need escape from death. We need immortality. As Psalm 49 says: "Truly no man can ransom himself or give to God the price of his life. . . ." Fill a wheelbarrow with your good deeds or your money, and go around the world and see who will sell you immortality or forgiveness. No, you can't buy immortality.

Another thing is that we don't deserve mercy. By our sins we have rebelled against God. We have sided with the enemy. But, no matter, we can count on God's mercy anyhow. What is mercy? Mercy is love put to use. It is serving love; it is forgiving love.

Let us look at the place of mercy in Revelation. Throughout the Old Testament God's mercy is stressed and repeated and recounted. The moment Adam and Eve fall God punishes them but also promises redemption. The Old Testament, particularly in the Psalms, is full of expressions of God's mercy. And we are told that His covenant with His people is practically mercy in essence because it is a gift of His love which they did not deserve. And we are told repeatedly that His mercy is everlasting.

In the story of Jonah, God expresses how much He longs for His people to renounce their sins and be healed. He sent Jonah to threaten the people's destruction and Jonah is waiting for this to happen. He wants his prophecy to be fulfilled, but God explains to Jonah that the prophecy of destruction was in the hope that the people would repent and God would save them (cf. Jon. 4:5 - 11).

In the New Testament we read in Paul's letter to Titus: "When the goodness and loving kindness of God our Savior appeared, he saved us not because of deeds done by us in righteousness, but in virtue of his own mercy" (Tit. 3:4 - 5). And Paul writes in Galatians that "if justification were through the law, then Christ died to no purpose" (Gal. 2:21). No, redemption and immortality are God's gifts of love. Mercy is not just a quality of our religion, it is its *heart*. It is the heart of Jesus. For what is Christmas but God's mercy come to us Incarnate in the person of His beloved Son, who is our love's Savior. He was made "sin" for us.

We find in the fourth chapter of the first letter of John, these words: "In this is love, not that we love God, but that He loved us and sent His Son to be the expiation of our sins" (Jn. 4:10). In the good shepherd and in the parable of the prodigal son, Jesus teaches us about the Father's love, and He Himself is an expression of the Father's love and mercy. Do you remember the man who came up to Jesus? He was a leper, and he said: "If you will, you can make me clean." And Jesus said: "I will — be clean" (Mk. 1:40 - 41). And He says it to us whenever we ask for His forgiveness and the healing from our impurities.

Mercy is such a great gift of God! It is one of His greatest favors. What would our creation profit us without His mercy that forgives and redeems us? What would this land be — this earth — to us repeating sinners without the sacrament of confession which makes it a land of beginning again? Is there anyone in this life who is so evil he cannot have God's forgiveness, if he wants it? To say *yes* would be blasphemy, for there is no one whose sin is stronger than God's forgiving love.

Let us remember that the best sign we have accepted God's forgiveness is that we fight sin in our lives and that we become forgiving ourselves. And let us close with this prayer:

> O Jesus, Josue, Your very Name means Savior, but it has no meaning except in us poor sinners who are helpless and hope-

less without You, as a cup is meaningless without content. Your Name has meaning when we cry to You, 'Save Us!' and You do. I cannot ransom myself. Ransom me. Be my Redemption. You are Savior and I saved. When I look at You crucified, Jesus, I can never doubt that You do and will redeem me. And I thank You in the words of Psalm 103: "Bless the Lord, O my soul; and all that is within me, bless his holy name! . . . as far as the east is from the west, so far does he remove our transgressions from us." Praise You, Jesus! May You be our Savior, our Redeemer, our happiness with the Father forever. Amen.

52. Death of a Christian

Is there something better than a fearful or a fateful attitude toward death? What are the positive aspects of dying?

They tell the story of this little boy who kept visiting his friend in his home. One day he exclaimed: "Every time I come your grandmother is reading the Bible!" And the other boy said, "Yes, she is preparing for the final exam!" That's one exam we all have to prepare for, and we prepare for it by preparing to die.

A friend of mine who was a chaplain in the Korean war described to me what I call the *Korean case*. The Chinese suddenly entered the war and they came storming down the peninsula like a tidal wave. The American Army was trapped. To a contingent of soldiers stationed between the Chinese and the retreating American Army the field commander issued the order, "Stand and die!" And they did. And they bought time for the rest of the American Army to escape the trap.

One day the great Commander-in-chief will say to each of us singly: "Stand and die!" And we will. For, as the Letter to the Hebrews tells us, "it is appointed that men die once and after death be judged" (Heb. 9:27).

What is death? From a natural point of view, death is the

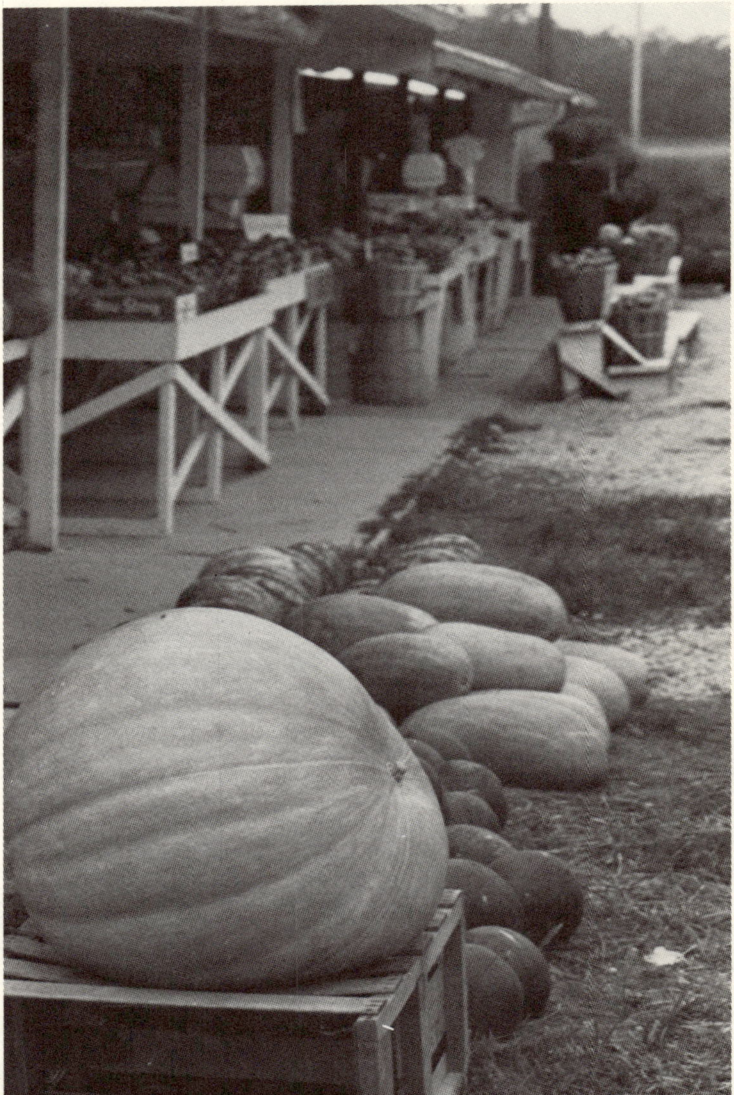

end of present bodily life. That is all we know from a scientific point of view. But what is death from a Christian point of view? From the revelation we know that death is a change of life, for in death life is changed, not taken away. Death is the continuation and completion of a process which we begin at baptism. Paul says: "You have died with Christ." We already died to many things at baptism, and our physical death is only a completion of the process. Furthermore, death can be defined as the only way to enter true life. And yet, the common attitudes toward death when it threatens are unchristian. First there is disbelief: "Death is now coming to me?" Then there is anger, and then bargaining with God, and finally, it is to be hoped, there is acceptance.

But the Christian attitude should be much better than that. When death comes I should have the attitude: "All my life has been a preparation for this; I now have it to do and I have to do it alone." And I will remember, it is to be hoped, that, as the Book of Wisdom says, "God did not make death" (Wis. 1:13). Death is a product of sin, the sin of man and the angels, and God will overcome it and restore life. A friend of mine had a father who died recently, and in facing his death he was more than resigned, he was expectant; he looked forward, he was curious, he viewed it with a child's wonder. He was also a little anxious, and he explained his anxiety. He said, "It's just that you have never done it before!"

One famous bishop, when asked how he felt as he was dying said: "Like a schoolboy going home for the holidays!" And Saint Paul said: "I long to be freed from this life and to be with Christ" (Phil. 1:23). And Jesus said: "I have a baptism to receive. What anguish I feel till it is over!" (Lk. 12:50). And when death came He said: "Father, into thy hands I commend my spirit."

That is the way to prepare for death. We spend time with Jesus in His dying. We learn how to die. We meditate on the passion. And when we go to Mass we celebrate His death and participate through the Eucharist in His resurrection. This is the secret of preparation for death, spending time with Jesus in His death and looking forward to Him in His resurrection.

Lord Jesus, You called Peter and invited him to come to You over the waters and he walked on the water but then he was afraid, and You said to him, "O man of little faith, why did you doubt?" Take away our fear of death. Give us the joy of coming to You. You have blazed the path; take away our fear of following You along it. Make me ready, and then call me and bid me come to You, to where you have prepared a place for me. Help me to believe firmly what You taught in Your parables: that death is only the means You employ to gather into the barns of eternal life the good crop that You have grown in us. Amen.

53. A Secret of Patience

Why is patience so hard to come by? How can we grow in patience?

If a preacher had to have perfectly the virtue he is going to preach about, there would probably be few sermons preached about patience, and certainly this reflection would not be written. But in struggling to develop patience, one may learn many things helpful to others. What I have learned in struggling with impatience is what I report here.

First of all, let me describe the good things patience produces and the evils impatience causes. Patience is the virtue that disposes a man to pursue his objectives despite suffering. When sorrows and vexations afflict us, impatience makes us tend, as Shakespeare puts it, "to take arms against a sea of troubles, / And by opposing end them. . . ." Patience takes a much different approach. Patience is the virtue that considers whether taking up such arms may not be worse than the sorrows and vexations. How often does husband or wife respond to the marriage partner with escalating anger and frustration that ultimately destroys the marriage itself? In protecting reason from being overturned by a mindless rush into foolish conduct, patience guards the attainment of our hopes. It prevents us from flinging ourselves off the precipice of obstacles and counsels us to climb down slowly. Impatience is irrationality. It destroys families, friendships, and nations. Patience is the virtue that delivers man's free spirit from this captivity. Patience is a brotherly virtue. Paul says: "Bear with one another and forgive whatever grievances you may have. Forgive, just as the Lord has forgiven you." Because it is a jealous guardian of reason, patience is an outpost of civilization. By it we lay down the tomahawk and take up the peace pipe. It takes strength to be patient, and therefore patience is the virtue of the strong. Nevertheless, the patient man is often considered weak by those who are ignorant of the true nature of patience.

In view of these reflections on what patience does and what impatience causes, let me draw some conclusions. One thing we have observed already is that patience is putting up with what we don't want. Behold, there is the reason why patience is so hard to come by! Who wants to put up with what he doesn't want? How can we ever gain patience when we put it that way? Well, let us look for motives. Our motive is this: Patience is a forgiving attitude toward another who does us harm or causes us suffering. Well, we have to develop this forgiving attitude if we are going to be Christians and if we are going to be saved, forgiven our own sins, and brought to eternal life. Jesus put on our lips the words: "Father . . . forgive us our trespasses as we forgive those who trespass against us." And Jesus said elsewhere that if we don't forgive, we won't be forgiven.

St. Paul gives us another lead and another motive. He says, "Love is patient." Well, if we want love, and I think we all want to grow in love, then we want to be patient because patience is one of the faces of love. Paul also says, "Love is not puffed up," and this exposes another vice of impatience. Impatience is the attitude by which we think our way is always superior to others' and is always right. So, if we develop lowliness and humility, we will grow in patience.

Patience is difficult. Even Jesus once exclaimed: "How long can I endure you?" (Mt. 17:17 NAT), thus revealing to us the difficulty of growing in patience. He also told us how to develop patience. He said: "There is no greater love than this: to lay down one's life for one's friends" (Jn. 15:13 NAT). Who of us has had to be so patient that we have had to lay down our life for our friends? But we do have to dispose ourselves to suffer for friends if we want to be patient with them.

Here is the greatest secret I have discovered with regard to patience: I have discovered the very word patience comes from the Latin word *patientia*, which means *willingness and readiness to suffer*. Where are we going to get that willingness and readiness? I know where I get it: by meditating on the passion of Jesus Christ. Every time I meditate on His passion and see how He has loved me and put up with my sins, I want to suffer with Him in order to help Him in the work of redemption, and so pay Him back a little for His love for me — pay Him back by loving Him and all other men. In this is, for me, the great secret of patience.

54. Death and Resurrection

Why does the death of a near one sometimes strike us as unreal?

I have had two conflicting experiences in the presence of death. I'm going to describe them and then try to find their meaning.

The first experience I have had at the death of a near and dear one is the unreality of death. It is as though death couldn't be — that this loved one couldn't be gone. It is as though death were an ugly mask worn by a lovely child on Halloween, and that any moment the game must be over and the ugly mask of death come off, and the beautiful face of life reappear.

And the second experience I have had, the contrary experience, is of the utter finality of death — as though death were "the strongest of all living things," as though there can be no more: Say "Hail and farewell," for you will never see your loved one again.

What are we to make of these two experiences: of the first, which confirms our faith, and of the second, which denies it? Let us examine each of the experiences in turn. First, we look at the experience of the unreality of death and we ask ourselves: Is this experience merely our effort to escape reality? Some undoubtedly make such efforts. They formulate preposterous funerals to pretend death did not happen — and they indulge in this escapism not because they believe in the resurrection but because they don't. And so the amateur psychologist in me says: This experience of the unreality of death is merely escapism — the shocked response of the nervous system — the inability to accept the loss.

Now this may well account for part of this experience of unreality, but my reason and judgment say it does not account for it all. And so I ask the obvious question: Is the source of the experience *the fact that death really is unreal?* As soon as that thought came to me, the man of God in me recognized it as the true answer. It is this answer that Sacred Scripture supports. The Book of Wisdom says: "Do not invite death by the error of your way of life . . . because God did not make death" (Wis. 1:12 - 14). Thus man's death did not come from the *God of nature*, so it is *unnatural.*

Where did death come from then? Jesus said: "The devil . . . brought death to man from the beginning, and has never based himself on truth" (Jn. 8:44 NAT). Therefore death seems unreal because it is *abnormal.* It stains life like a blotch on a white dress; it is as out of place in life as a tall building standing alone in the middle of an endless desert. Neither death nor the tall building seem quite real. The reason is that neither blends with nature because neither is from nature, and so neither looks natural.

If we experience death as unreal, why do we also experience it as so final? Here are my thoughts on that. Recently I was at a funeral, and in the presence of that dead body all the consolations of philosophy turned to gibberish, and all the theology of theologians not based on Scripture blew away like cobwebs in a cyclone, for the devil's work is stronger than man's, and death is his work. But then my thought turned to Jesus Christ who said: "I am the resurrection and the life." It is He in whom I hope, for in that hope I am not trying to wring life out of an idea, as philosophers tend to do. No, by my faith I seek life from Him who is life and who created life and who promised resurrection life to us, and who rose from the dead to have it for us and who will return to give it to us.

Now we can understand why death looks so final even though it is not. Death brags to us and inflates itself and pretends to what it is not because it is the work of that braggart the devil. It pretends a permanence it does not have because it is the offspring of a liar and the father of lies. Death appears to be permanent but the Son of God said that "the hour is coming when all who are in the tombs will hear (the Son of Man's) voice and come forth, those who have done good, to the resurrection of life, and those who have done evil, to the resurrection of judgment" (Jn. 5:28 - 29).

These words of the Lord give us a second reason why death looks so final. It is a punishment for sin, and those who continue in sin and die in sin will live forever in a kind of death which the Book of Revelation calls "the second death" (2:11).

The words of the Lord also tell us why we experience death as unreal. We are simply tasting our own immortality. The poet Wordsworth even named this type of experience. He called it "Intimations of Immortality."

Here is the situation then: Death looks so final that many say it is final. But death has never really said: "I am final!"

No, the claim that death is final is man's claim, while the claim that life is final is God's claim. In the Book of Revelation Jesus says: "There is nothing to fear. I am the First and the Last and the One who lives. Once I was dead but now I live — forever and ever" (1:17 - 18 NAT). And when He promised the Eucharist He said: "He who eats my flesh and drinks my blood has eternal life, and I will raise him up at the last day" (Jn. 6:54).

At the funeral I spoke of I went to the altar and consecrated and ate the body and blood of Christ and fed it to the people. This was my answer. Death is a transient but God is eternal and through the slain and risen body of His Son He gives us life that puts an end to death forever. And so one day you and I will have the joy of meeting in "the resurrection of the body and life everlasting." Amen.

55. Who's Afraid of the Golden Rule?

Do we avoid practicing the golden rule because we are afraid of it? What does this fear tell us about ourselves?

Mike was being beaten unmercifully by Jim in a chess game, so he said: "Jim, why don't you do unto others as you'd have them do unto you?" And Jim replied: "Sorry, Mike, but in chess my rule is: Do unto others before they do unto you!"

Now I would not argue with Jim's rule for a chess game, but unfortunately I have heard some people apply the same rule to the game of life: Do unto others before they do unto you. But these people are not our guides. We have one guide, one Lord and Master, the Christ. And in the Gospel of Matthew he gave us what has long been known as the golden rule: "Do to others what you would have others do to you. This sums up the law and the prophets" (7:12). Can you imagine the immense value Jesus Christ is assigning to this eleven-word rule? It contains in capsule form what the law and the prophets were trying to teach men to be and to do.

Many hundreds of years later the Earl of Chesterfield declared: "Do as you would be done by is the surest method of pleasing." In other words, the golden rule not only pleases God; it pleases men and makes us popular. Therefore, we have a natural as well as a God-given motive for practicing it. Why then do we neglect it? Is it simply that we are selfish and do not want to pay the cost of practicing the golden rule? No doubt that is the case with some persons; they know their problem, and it is up to them to deal with it. But I believe that in many cases the obstacle to our practicing the golden rule is hidden, so that we not only don't practice the golden rule, but we don't know why we don't and we don't know what to do about it. The purpose of this reflection is to surface the hidden obstacles to practicing the golden rule, so that we can do something about them.

Let us begin by examining the golden rule: It directs us to do to another what we would like done to us; but we have to add, "That is, what we would like done to us if we were the other person." To bring this out I adapt an old Indian saying to my purpose: "You don't know what you would like done if you were that other person until you have walked for a mile in that other person's moccasins!"

Now how do we walk for a mile in another person's moccasins? We do it by using our imaginations. Einstein said somewhere that imagination is as important as knowledge. That's because the imagination can create new knowledge for us. For example, the husband should examine his attitude toward his wife by seeing if he would like his conduct if he were on the receiving end of it; and the wife should imagine how she would be pleased with her way of acting if she were the husband. And children should imagine being their own parents, and parents their own children, to see if they are following the golden rule. And so with other relationships too.

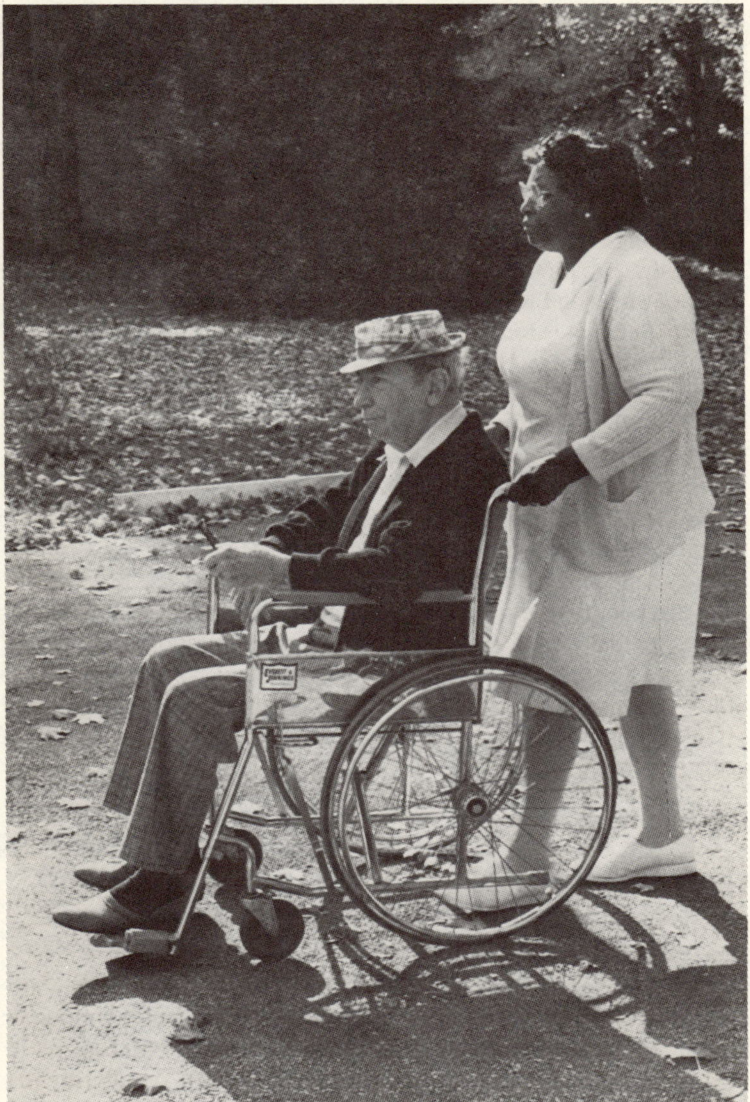

If we are aware of the need to think about the experiences and preferences of others and don't do it, it may be that we are self-centered persons. The self-centered person isn't exactly selfish, because the selfish person really doesn't care about others. The self-centered person wants to care, but he is so busy thinking about himself he rarely gets around to caring. We can overcome this obstacle to the golden rule by consciously fighting the tendency to think about ourselves.

Now I go on to the third obstacle. Sometimes we are afraid to face someone who is angry with us, so that when we see him we pretend we don't, and quickly go the other way. Well, I think many of us act in this evasive way toward the golden rule too. We fear it, and avoid it, and don't know quite why. By thinking it over, I have found two reasons for that fear in myself. The first reason is that since I sometimes make unreasonable demands on others, I'm afraid the golden rule allows them to make unreasonable demands on me. But surely that is not what Christ meant by the golden rule. He said we should do what we would want others to do to us. Now to the extent that we are virtuous ourselves, we would not make unreasonable demands on others — nor will we let them make unreasonable demands on us. Sometimes even Jesus said No. So if we fear the golden rule, what that may tell us is that we are making unreasonable demands on others, and are afraid the tables will be turned.

The second reason I have found in myself that makes me fear the golden rule is that I am afraid, not of what my neighbor will ask of me, but of what my God will ask of me. You see, I've never succeeded in habitually trusting Jesus who said: "Take my yoke upon your shoulders. . . . For my yoke is easy and my burden light" (Mt. 11:29).

But let me tell you of one case in which I trusted Him completely. When I was a boy I appreciated priests tremendously. I was a sinner, and they brought me forgiveness and peace in confession. I was hungry for God, and they brought me the sacredness of the Mass, and fed me with Holy Communion.

What they did for me I appreciated so much, I wanted to do the same for others. So I took on me the yoke of Christ's priesthood, with joy and not fear. And since then I have been doing for others what so many priests had done for me, and I have found joy in it, and to this extent at least I have practiced the golden rule and learned how golden it is.

And so I close with one suggestion. Each person should look for one thing in which he can practice the golden rule happily, and start there. It has a habit of spreading to everything else.

56. Big Little Things

What is the importance of little things? Do humdrum days have an eternal significance?

One day I climbed barefooted down a stairwell. Suddenly my foot flared up in an explosion of pain. A bee had stung me. The bee was little, and its stinger was littler, but that little bee became a big event in my life that day.

At Mt. Palomar there is a two-hundred-inch telescope. Little stars look big to the astronomers there. But the telescope does not exaggerate. In reality the stars are much bigger than it makes them look to the astronomers.

Most of the time most of us live lives where everything seems small and unimportant, and we begin to feel just as small and just as unimportant. We get bored, and we even get desperate for something important in our lives.

I would like to level a two-hundred-inch telescope of thought on the little things in our lives. We may learn that in reality they are not small at all. We may discover the bigness of little things.

There are people who have realized the bigness of little things. I will mention three. The first is Jesus. He had a world to save, and yet He spent thirty of His thirty-three years in the ordinary quiet little affairs of a small-town life. The second is a theologian named John Courtney Murray. His involvement in world affairs led to his picture being featured on the cover of *Time* magazine. And yet when his students went to him for advice he was as gracious with his time as if he had nothing to do. The third person is a young woman who never did anything but little things all her short life. And yet less than thirty years later Pope Benedict XV canonized her *Saint* Thérèse of Lisieux, and said that he wanted word of her and her little way to spread over the whole world. And it has.

What did Jesus and these two followers of His know about the importance of little things that we don't? How did they learn to find such a wise balance between big and little things?

Let me give some examples of the problem, and then propose the solution which Jesus and His faithful followers suggest. First, an example in my life. I have a missionary heart. I want to preach the Gospel far and wide. Yet my life is often taken up with little things, as one day when an old priest came into my room troubled in conscience because of scruples. I spent an hour with him, and yet he was back the next day and the next. Sometimes when I spend time this way, I grow impatient for greater affairs, and yet I recognize failure there.

I see the same failure in the lives of others. Some married men are always laying grandiose plans that are never productive. In the meantime they scorn the ordinary little job they need to support their families. Some wives are so concerned with what they consider important affairs that they neglect their homes and families until they go to ruin.

What are Jesus and those two followers of His trying to tell us? I think they are trying to tell us that if we take care of the little things the big things will take care of themselves. Jesus said: "He who is faithful in a very little is faithful also in much" (Lk. 16:10). I think Jesus is trying to make us understand that the house of love should be the one big thing in our lives, but that it can exist only if it is patiently built over the years with the little bricks of faithfulness and truth and selfless service.

It is true that if we neglect the big things we will not make our lives what we ought; but if we neglect the little things, we will not make ourselves what we ought. We can do the big things from many motives, such as the desire for prestige; but we can consistently do the little things only from the motive of love for our loved ones. And the word of God says: "If I . . . have not love, I am nothing" (cf. 1 Cor. 13:2).

The person who wants to do nothing but big things gets very busy. The poet George Herbert said everyone can love except the busied man. Jesus did little things well because He loved people.

There is magic in little things. A little diamond can be worth more than a carload of other things. What then about a whole field of diamonds? What of a whole life shining with the beauty of little deeds done as God asked? Count no thing small — not even one gray hair — if it turned gray in the service of God and His people.

We are told that Abraham served a meal to angels unawares. Is a meal served to your husband, to your children, to a hungry man in kindness, a lesser thing in the eyes of God? Jesus said: "What you do to others you do to me." How many little deeds of kindness have been done for Jesus unawares?

Why are little things so important? — because God wants them of us, and that is no little thing? Abraham Lincoln once said: "God must love the common people. He made so many of them." Someone has said: "The trouble with life is that it is so daily!" That's true. It can be boring to do little things. It's a grind. Could that be why Jesus prepared us by saying: "If anyone wants to be a follower of mine, let him renounce himself and take up his cross every day and follow me"? The only thing that resolves the tedium of little things is a big love.

There is something special about little deeds of love done for a lifetime. That lifetime hides its heroism from all but God. It gives Him the glory.

In speaking about the heights of love, Jesus said: "Greater love than this no man has, that a man lay down his life for his friends" (Jn. 15:13). I think that to lay down our lives over the years in little ways of service can be harder than to lay them down in one swift moment of bravery. That means that what others tend to view as lives of quiet desperation just may be the successes of the century, as was the life of Thérèse of Lisieux, the Little Flower. For doing little things with love can make us big saints.

57. A Saint in the Making

Would you like to meet a potential saint living today? Can such a meeting be arranged in a way that will change your life?

I would like first to introduce you to a reluctant Saint of four centuries ago, and then to a potential but reluctant saint of today. The reluctant Saint of four centuries ago was a Spanish youth named Francis. One fateful day there hobbled into his life a lame ex-soldier named Ignatius. By word and example the ex-soldier tried to interest Francis in meeting a potential saint. The potential saint Ignatius wanted Francis to meet was Francis.

The introduction of Francis the sinner to Francis the saint went poorly. Francis was a university student, but he was more interested in athletics than academics, and he was least of all interested in sainthood.

Biographers have summarized the soldier's strategy by saying that he continued to repeat to Francis the words of Jesus: "What does it profit a man if he gain the whole world but suffer the loss of his own soul?" (Mk. 8:37). But Ignatius seemed to get nowhere. Yet the grain of wheat that is Christ was growing in Francis' soul, because four years later he began to change his whole way of life.

He who had been so reluctant to be a saint began praying and doing penance and making a retreat. He then became a priest. Years passed, and he still had to fight his own passions to live as a celibate, but now he was glad to fight any battle for Christ.

He began exhausting himself with hard priestly work. One night he woke and said to his priest-companion: "Jesus! How crushed and fatigued I feel! Do you know what I dreamt? — that I was trying to hoist an Indian on my shoulders, and he was such a deadly weight I couldn't lift him."

Not long after that he was sent to India as a missionary. In India he baptized so many people that once he could no longer lift his arm to pour the water. He labored to help his people make a better living as well as live a better life. He cared for their bodies as well as their souls. He tried to bring change by changing himself. He worked harder and lived poorer than the poor he wanted to make a little better off. His heart was so great he would have liked to change the world, but his love was so real that at least he changed himself.

He worked miracles, but the greatest was the miracle of his love that changed him from an athletic playboy to an athlete of Christ, racing to any place he could better serve God and his people. He went to India, then Japan, then set out for China. This reluctant Saint died, no longer reluctant, on the island of Sancian, off the coast of China — but not before he had become the radiant apostle of the Jesuits, the glory of the missions, and a Saint. To millions still today he is the beloved St. Francis Xavier.

Now let me introduce, with a long windup, a potential saint of our day. First, the windup: One of the two most popular talks I have given on the Sacred Heart radio program was entitled: "I am a Sinner." The point of it was not only that I am a sinner, but that you are a sinner. The point was that to be saved by Jesus the Savior we have to confess we are sinners who need His salvation. The favorable response to the talk proved that it's easy for most of us to admit that we are sinners.

That's the windup; now here's the pitch right over the plate: You the sinner are also you the potential saint whom I want you to meet. As the soldier introduced Francis the sinner to Francis the potential saint, I introduce you the sinner to you the potential saint.

In doing this I am only handing on the genuine Christian message. I am not playing games. Jesus said: "You . . . must be perfect, as your heavenly Father is perfect" (Mt. 5:48). And St. Paul wrote that "God chose us in [Christ] to be holy and blameless in his sight, to be full of love" (Eph. 1:4 NAT). And when he wrote a letter to the Christians at Philippi, he addressed it as follows: "Paul and Timothy . . . to all the *saints* in Christ Jesus who are at Philippi . . ." (Phil. 1:1).

Now let me go back to St. Francis and the example of the saints. Most saints are ex-sinners, and therefore the saint gives us a great help because, as an ex-sinner, he is to us sinners what an abstaining alcoholic is to drinking alcoholics — the proof that it can be done, and the challenge to say, "If he did it, I can do it!" And that is what I am asking you to say. You a sinner can become and are called to become you a saint. Now that you a sinner have met you who are called to be a saint, may God help you to grow into the likeness of Christ to the full. This is my prayer for you and for myself. Let us pray for one another, that we may one day go marching in and fill up the halls of heaven with the saints whom Christ has called to share His life forever.